Castles of Aberdeenshire

Castles of Aberdeenshire

HISTORICAL AND DESCRIPTIVE NOTICES
(1887)

partly reprinted from
Sir Andrew Leith Hay's
Castellated Architecture of Aberdeenshire

*with
pen and ink drawings
by*
Wm. Taylor

The Grimsay Press

The Grimsay Press
An imprint of Zeticula
57, St Vincent Crescent
Glasgow
G3 8NQ
Scotland
http://www.thegrimsaypress.co.uk

First published in 1887 by D. Wyllie & Son, Aberdeen.

This edition first published in 2011

ISBN 978-1-84530-113-2

PREFACE.

THE text of the present work is to a considerable extent a reprint of Sir ANDREW LEITH HAY'S "Castellated Architecture of Aberdeenshire," published in 1849, which has been out of print for some years, and is now seldom to be met with. All the articles have undergone a careful revision, some of them have been considerably extended, and the following have been specially written or re-written for the present volume, viz., those on Aboyne, Balfluig, Balquhain, Barra, Castle Fraser, Dudwick, Fyvie, Huntly, Inverugie, Kinnaird, Knock, Midmar, Udny, and Westhall. Of these fourteen castles only Balquhain, Castle Fraser, Fyvie, Huntly, Udny, and Westhall were represented in the former work. The aim, throughout, has been to present, in brief compass, the more interesting points connected with the various centres of influence and action in a district peculiarly rich in historic associations. Around not a few of these old castles have gathered the forces on the issues of whose warfare the fortunes of families, and even the fate of dynasties, have turned. The wars of Robert Bruce, of Queen Mary, and of the Covenanters, had several of their most momentous conflicts within this region; it was here that the Jacobite rising of 1715 had its inception and first developments; and Aberdeenshire also had its share, though a secondary one, in the final struggle on behalf of the Stuarts in 1745. To name the battles of Inverurie and Barra, of Culblean and Harlaw, of Corrichie, Craibstane, and Tullyangus, of Aberdeen and Alford, is to enumerate so many of the landmarks of Scottish or local history. To these and many other events of a stirring epoch, the venerable strongholds whose configuration or remains are depicted in this volume, are intimately related.

CONTENTS.

	PAGE		PAGE
ABERGELDIE,	1	HUNTLY,	71
ABOYNE,	6	INVERCAULD,	83
BALBITHAN,	10	INVERUGIE,	87
BALQUHAIN,	11	KILDRUMMIE,	100
BALFLUIG,	14	KINNAIRD,	109
BALMORAL,	17	KNOCK,	3
BARRA,	21	KNOCKHALL,	112
CORSE,	23	LEITH-HALL,	113
CAIRNBULG,	110	LESLIE,	115
CRAIGIEVAR,	27	LICKLYHEAD,	117
CRAIG,	30	MELDRUM,	119
CRAIGSTON,	35	MIDMAR,	123
DRUM,	37	MONYMUSK,	126
DRUMINNOR,	43	NEWE,	129
DUDWICK,	48	PITCAPLE,	132
DUNNIDEER,	45	RAVENSCRAIG,	139
FORBES (CASTLE),	105	TERPERSIE,	141
FORMARTINE,	54	TOLQUHON,	143
FRASER (CASTLE),	50	TOWIE,	146
FYVIE,	57	TOWIE BARCLAY,	148
GLENBUCKET,	65	UDNY,	157
HALLFOREST,	15	WESTHALL,	160
HARTHILL,	67		

LIST OF ILLUSTRATIONS.

	PAGE		PAGE
ABERGELDIE AND KNOCK,	1	HUNTLY, Fireplace,	78
ABOYNE,	6	INVERCAULD,	84
BALBITHAN AND BALQUHAIN,	10	INVERUGIE,	88
BALFLUIG AND HALLFOREST,	14	KILDRUMMIE AND CASTLE FORBES,	100
BALMORAL,	18	KINNAIRD AND CAIRNBULG,	110
BARRA,	22	KNOCKHALL,	112
CORSE,	24	LEITH-HALL,	114
CRAIGIEVAR,	28	LESLIE,	116
CRAIG,	30	LICKLYHEAD,	118
CRAIGSTON,	36	MELDRUM,	120
DRUM,	38	MIDMAR,	124
DRUMINNOR AND DUNNIDEER,	44	MONYMUSK,	126
DUDWICK,	48	NEWE,	130
FORMARTINE,	54	PITCAPLE,	132
FRASER (CASTLE),	50	RAVENSCRAIG,	140
FYVIE,	58	TERPERSIE,	142
Do. Staircase,	64	TOLQUHON,	144
GLENBUCKET,	66	TOWIE,	146
HARTHILL,	68	TOWIE BARCLAY,	156
HUNTLY,	72	UDNY,	158
Do. Entrance Door,	76	WESTHALL,	160

I.
ABERGELDIE.

ABERGELDIE Castle, formerly the property of the Mowats but now of the Gordons, is romantically placed on the south bank of the Dee at the mouth of the Geldie, a small tributary of that river. Extensive woods, growing to the summits of the lofty eminences to the south-east of the castle, add to the effect of a scene naturally picturesque, and the summits of Loch-na-gar, seen in the distance, form a consistent and grand termination to a Highland landscape. The birch woods that surround the castle are celebrated in the well known Scottish ballad of "The Birks of Abergeldie;" and the romantic story of the encounter of the Mowats and the Camerons of Brux, gives an interest to the early history of the venerable castle, of which the former were then the proprietors. The tradition is, that to decide their quarrel the parties agreed to meet on the hill of Drumgaudrum, in the parish of Kildrummie, each to be accompanied by eleven horsemen; that the laird of Abergeldie, in bad faith, arrived with a foot soldier behind each of his party, and in this disproportioned number they were on the field of conflict, before the Camerons became aware of the treachery practised, and when it was too late for them to evade the unequal conquest. The Camerons engaged with resolution, and were stimulated not only by their feudal hatred, but by an earnest desire to revenge the deceit so unworthily practised. This fight terminated the male line of the Camerons of Brux, the laird being slain, leaving an only daughter, and on the side of Mowat, his two sons, with twelve others, were left dead on the field.

Catherine Cameron, surrounded by admirers, but feeling indignation at the treachery by which her father had been deprived of life, declared that her hand should be bestowed on him who sued her favour after having slain the laird of Abergeldie. It is related that a rivalry existed in the family of Lord Forbes, and that each of his four sons sought to gain her affections, but upon her declaration being made known, Robert, the second of these, alone determined to gain the prize.

With this intent, he challenged Mowat to meet him at Badenyon, in the parish of Glenbucket, where they assembled, in command of about an equal number of clansmen and retainers. Robert Forbes addressed his adversary, and proposed a single combat, to terminate their differences without a great loss of blood, which a general engagement of the parties would inevitably produce; to this proposal the fiery and reckless Mowat assented, and the combatants closed in deadly strife. The result was for some time doubtful, but at length the laird of Abergeldie fell mortally wounded, and his young and gallant opponent returned to Kildrummie to claim his bride, and having married Catherine Cameron, became the ancestor of the Forbeses of Brux.

Sir Alexander Gordon, who was the first laird of Abergeldie of that name, married the daughter of the Earl of Erroll, by whom he had two sons and four daughters; his elder son, George, and the second, William, laird of Netherdale; his eldest daughter who married Lord Lovat; the second, Mortimer of Craigievar; the third, Ogilvy of Clova; and the fourth, Garden of Dorlaithers. Sir Alexander was succeeded by his elder son, who married Grizel, daughter of the Earl of Buchan. Their son, Alexander, succeeded, and married Janet, the heiress of Leith of Barns, and the widow of the laird of Meldrum, by whom he had three sons. Of these, Alexander became the fourth laird of Abergeldie; he married the daughter of Irvine of Drum, and had a family of six sons and six daughters. Their fourth son, George, was killed at the battle of Glenlivat in 1594. The eldest, Alexander, became the fifth laird of Abergeldie, and died without heirs. His brother, William, succeeded: he married the daughter of Andrew, Lord Gray. They had five sons and two daughters, the elder of whom married Donaldson of Monaltrie, the second, Gray of Shivas. The sixth laird died in 1630, when his eldest son, Alexander, became the seventh laird of Abergeldie, of the name of Gordon. John, his son, succeeded to the estate, and married a daughter of Ross of Kilravock: but having no family, the succession devolved upon his sister, Rachel, who married Captain Charles Gordon, son of Peter Gordon of Minmore, by Janet, the daughter of Sir Alexander Gordon of Cluny, by whom he had a son and successor. Peter Gordon married, first, Margaret, daughter of Peter Strachan of Edinburgh, and, secondly, Elizabeth, daughter of Lord Gray, by whom he had a daughter, married to Hunter of Burnside. This laird married, thirdly, Margaret, the daughter of Sir George Foulis of Dunipace, by Janet, daughter of Sir John Cunningham of Caprington, and sister to Sir Archibald Foulis, executed at Carlisle in 1745. He was succeeded by his son, Charles, who married the daughter of Hunter of Burnside; their eldest son, Peter, a Captain in the 81st Highland Regiment, married, first, Mary, daughter to John Forbes of Blackford, by whom he had a daughter, who died in 1802; and secondly, Elizabeth, daughter of Mr. Leith of Freefield, and, dying without heirs, was succeeded by his brother, David, a merchant in London, who died in the year 1831, and whose son, Michael Francis, succeeded to the estate. In 1860 he died, and was succeeded by his brother, Admiral Robert Gordon, who dying unmarried, the estate came into possession of his nephew, Hugh Mackay Gordon, Esquire, the present representative of the family.

The castle is now part of the royal demesnes being held by Her Majesty on lease from the proprietor, and has for sometime past formed the Highland residence of the Prince and Princess of Wales. Following upon a recent renewal of the lease, Her Majesty has erected in place of the somewhat dangerous cradle that did service for many years, a suspension bridge across the river giving access to the castle from the north bank.

KNOCK CASTLE.

THE picturesque old ruin of Knock (Knoc or Cnoic, literally Knoll) occupies a commanding position on the ridge of Ardmeanach, about a mile to the west of the confluence of the Muick with the Dee. Overlooking a long stretch of the valleys of these rivers and the lower Gairn, its importance in the olden days of feuds and forays was very considerable. Before the castle was built, the remains of which still arrest the eye, another tower had stood for centuries not far from the same unique site, its origin dating back to the time of the ancient earls or mormaers of Mar. Early in the fourteenth century the lands of Glenmuick were held by the Bissets; and later on they passed successively into the families of Fraser, of Keith, Earl Marischal, and of Gordon, Earl of Huntly. At one time the fortalice of Knock was held by the Durwards. It was also the seat of a royal garrison charged with the duty of maintaining the supreme authority in the Deeside Highlands. In those days the actual master of the Knock would be changed from time to time according to circumstances or the King's pleasure. After the advent of the Gordons, as narrated elsewhere in this volume, these changes ceased. Alexander, the third Earl of Huntly, who commanded at Flodden and was married to a sister of the King, appointed one of his sons to the command of this stronghold. This Earl, who had been Lieutenant-General of the northern half of Scotland, was succeeded by his son, George, a great statesman as well as soldier, one of whose acts, as Lord Chancellor of Scotland, was to confer the Castle and Lands of Knock upon a brother of Gordon of Abergeldie, a relative of his own. The rivalry between Huntly and the Regent Murray, and between the Catholic and Protestant parties of which for a time they were respectively the heads, belongs to the domain of general history. First on being created Earl of Mar, and secondly on being made Earl of Murray, the Regent carried this rivalry into the heart of the Gordon country. Huntly exerted himself to strengthen his interest in the north, put the various fortresses under his authority, into a condition of repair and defence, and caused others to be erected; and at Knock as elsewhere, preparations were made to uphold the Gordon standard. In the autumn of 1562 he marshalled his retainers and allies at Corrichie on the Hill of Fare. The battle ended in a disaster to the cause of the Gordons, in Huntly's death (or murder), and in many of his followers being taken prisoners. Many of the Forbeses were nominally under the Gordon standard, but when the battle came on they stood aside, and on the following day they made their submission to the Regent. From this and other causes bad blood arose or was aggravated between the two families that held nearly all the upper parts of West Aberdeenshire. Of the feuds between the Gordons and Forbeses many tales, more or less mythical, have been handed down in song or oral tradition. Some of these concern the Knock.

The family feud prevailed in all its intensity between Henry Gordon, second laird of Knock, and Alexander Forbes of Strathgirnock, whose property intervened between Knock and the Gordon domain of Abergeldie. According to tradition they quarrelled about a bridge across the Girnock; they also quarrelled about the cattle of their respective retainers which sometimes strayed or were driven across the marches, and were not regarded as a sacred kind of property. Personal encounters between the two lairds and their followers occasionally took place. So bitter was the feud between the Gordons and Forbeses at this time, that Farquharson of Castleton, who was of the Gordon connection, put away his wife because she was a niece of Lord Forbes; and the Master of Forbes divorced himself from a daughter of the house of Huntly. Nine years after Corrichie there was a great fight between the two families at Tillyangus. One of the chief men among the Forbeses in this battle, as also in that of Crabestane, Aberdeen, a few weeks afterwards, was the laird of Strathgirnock. At Crabestane he was captured by Alister Gordon, brother of Knock; and with many more of the Forbeses he was imprisoned for a time at Sir Adam Gordon's castle of Auchindoun. His lands during his absence had been in process of being merged in the Gordon properties by which they were surrounded, but he succeeded in regaining possession. Henry Gordon of Knock was killed, along with several of his neighbours, in a revengeful and cattle-lifting raid of the Clan Chattan, in which some of the Forbeses were supposed to be concerned. His brother, Alexander, who succeeded him, is said to have built the still existing castle of Knock—the fate of his predecessor and the troublous state of the times strongly suggesting the necessity for an impregnable stronghold. But he did not long live to enjoy the security it afforded against his foes. The tradition is that after a period of peace or truce, his seven sons while casting peats one day were caught unarmed by a party of Forbeses under Strathgirnock, and brutally put to death; and that Gordon himself, on hearing the tidings, fell down and breathed his last. The criminal jurisdiction of the last Earl and first Marquis of Huntly was exercised at this time by Alexander Gordon of Abergeldie, the fourth laird in the succession already mentioned. Forbes was condemned and summarily executed; his lands were annexed to those of Abergeldie, to which also the lands and castle of Knock were added by right of inheritance. So long as it continued to be inhabited Knock Castle was a seat of the Abergeldie family, or tenanted by particular members of that family. It is now the property of the Prince of Wales, having been purchased along with the Birkhall estate in 1848 from Mr. Gordon of Abergeldie.

II.

ABOYNE.

ABOYNE Castle, the principal seat of the Marquis of Huntly, though the greater part of it is more than two centuries old, is a spacious structure suited to modern conditions and little suggestive of those of a remote antiquity. It is finely situated amid Lowland surroundings but looking out on a picturesque Highland vista, and is to all intents and purposes a residential mansion having little in common with the military strongholds of former days. The situation which it occupies is such, indeed, that it may at one time have had the protection of a moat and drawbridge, but the building itself, as well as its location, betokens reposeful tranquility and an absence of the turbulence and conflict amidst which the castellated architecture of Aberdeenshire had its origin and development.

Towards the middle of the thirteenth century Walter Bisset was Lord of Aboyne and entertained Queen Joanna at the Castle. During the royal visit to Deeside the Earl of Athole was burnt to death at Haddington, and Bisset, between whom and the Earl there had been a feud, was suspected of being the instigator of the murder. He tried to clear himself at Edinburgh, but in the end he found it convenient to retire to England where he enjoyed the protection of Henry III., who was the brother of the Scottish Queen. Half a century later—in 1296—Edward I. of England in returning from his expedition to Morayshire sent some of his officers with a detachment of men to visit Aboyne Castle and bring away charters or other documents upon which they could lay their hands. A new charter of the lands of Aboyne was granted by King Robert Bruce to another Walter Bisset who seems to have been in his time the principal personage in Deeside, and a confirmatory charter was granted in the next reign to Thomas Bisset the last of the male line of that family. By the marriage of the heiress of the Bissets with Sir Alexander Fraser, nephew of Bruce the "arrearage and annuals of Aboyne," with the extensive properties, passed into the hands of the Frasers, and thence—also by marriage, in

Aboyne Castle.

the next generation—they were transferred first to the Keiths and to the Gordons. Alexander Gordon, first Earl of Huntly married Lady Jane Keith, heiress of Aboyne and a relative of his own, and through this marriage obtained possession of the castle and estate. Lady Jane died without issue but the lands had passed irrevocably into the possession of Huntly, who after his second marriage, with Elizabeth Crichton, obtained a charter in the following terms:—"To Alexander, Earl of Huntly, and the descendants and heirs between said Alexander and Elizabeth Countess of Huntly, born or to be born; whom failing, to the true, legitimate, and nearest heirs whomsoever of the said Alexander, All and whole the lands of Cluny, Tulch, Abyn, Glentanyr, and Glenmuck."* The Earl of Huntly when in the north resided principally in Strathbogie; and Aboyne Castle appears to have been found and left by him in a condition of decay. On the marriage of Adam Gordon, second son of the second Earl of Huntly with the heiress to the earldom of Sutherland, the barony of Aboyne was assigned to them, but the castle being in ruins they resided at Ferrar, some little distance to the west. They had only a life tenancy, however, the lands being attached by a fresh charter to "the barony and earldom of Huntly in all time to come." The object of this charter, indeed, was to prevent the recurrence of such a contingency as that which transferred the property from the Keiths to the Gordons, for when the charter was granted (1506) the succession of Lady Elizabeth to the dignity of Countess of Sutherland in her own right was distinctly in prospect, and in point of fact she did succeed to it nine years later. The Sutherland peerage was not to be enriched by any portion of the territorial patrimony of the earldom of Huntly—the Earl took good care of that.

For another century and more the history of Aboyne Castle is a blank—the Deeside residence of the heads of the Gordon family being first the fortified castle of Loch Kinnord, and afterwards the mansion of Kandychyle (or Dee Castle), built by the first Marquis of Huntly. In 1644, three years after Kandychyle had been destroyed by fire while in the possession of a tenant, the Marquis of that time summoned his retainers to Aboyne in preparation for the struggle with the Covenanters. At the head of a thousand men, two hundred of them on horseback, he proceeded to Aberdeen to await the issue of events. He soon saw the struggle to be hopeless, and on the approach of the Marquis of Argyle, the Earl Marischal, and his own son, Lord Gordon, with a force 6000 strong, he disbanded his retainers, and went for a time into retirement. Argyle proceeded up

* Michie's "Loch Kinnord," pp. 69-70.

Deeside, and quartered a body of eight hundred men upon the Huntly estates, collecting such rents as they could exact at the same time. These eight hundred were called the "Cleansers," because they "cleansed" all the country of whatever could be consumed or carried away. According to Spalding, "they plundered and spulzied the house of Aboyne and the house of Abergeldie, with their ground; they spulzied and plundered to haill Birse, Cromar, Glentanar, Glenmuick, and left neither horse, sheep, nolt, ky, nor four-footed beast in all these brave countries; nor victuals, corn, goods, nor gear that they might lay their hands upon; and seeing they could not live longer in those harried bounds, they got orders and moved home," after a memorable two months' stay. Within a few weeks the Covenanters split into two parties—Montrose going over to the King, while Argyle continued to hold the field. A protracted conflict between the rival parties ensued, with varying results, but in the end with heavy loss to the Gordon family. After the Restoration, however, some recompense was made when Charles Gordon, fourth but now eldest surviving son of the Marquis of Huntly who perished on the scaffold in Edinburgh, was raised to the peerage as Earl of Aboyne, and obtained a charter conveying to him the lands and lordship from which his title was derived. The first Countess of Aboyne was Margaret Irvine of Drum commemorated in the touching ballad of "Bonny Peggy Irvine." Some years after her death the Earl married Elizabeth Lyon, daughter of the Earl of Strathmore; he administered the Huntly estates during the long minority of his nephew, the Marquis; he was a man of great energy and influence, and not without literary power. By him the older portion of the castle now standing was built, about the year 1671. This is the left or western wing. For the time when it was erected the building was very commodious; and with the east wing, added by the fifth Earl in 1801 in the same style of architecture, it is still justly regarded as one of the most spacious residences in the north. There are finer houses not a few, so far as architecture is concerned, but few can vie with it in suitability for the reception and entertainment of a large party of guests. The latest accession to the massive pile dates from 1869 when the old wing containing kitchen and other accessory departments were replaced by a new granite structure of simple yet elegant design in keeping with the general character of the building.

In the days of Mar's insurrection Aboyne Castle was a centre of political interest, the Earl taking part with the Jacobites in their hopeless enterprise. His son and successor sympathised with the rising of 1745, but was still a minor at the time of its inception and by the prudent intervention of his friends he was got to Paris on the plea of finishing his education and there remained until the crisis had passed over. In after days he became a leader in agricultural improvement, planted extensively, and built, it is said, no less than forty miles of stone fences of more than five feet high.* For several generations Aboyne has been by far the most important seat on Deeside east of Balmoral, and its history has been in no small degree connected with that of the great district of which it is the centre.

* Michie's "Loch Kinnord," p. 111.

III.

BALBITHAN.

THE turretted mansion house of Balbithan is situated in the parish of Keith-hall, and removed a considerable distance from the site of the more ancient residence of the family, which stood at Old Balbithan, near the Don and opposite to the Royal Burgh of Kintore. It is related that one of the old lairds of Balbithan, in days when neither life nor property were safe in Scotland, was so disgusted at a shot being fired from Hallforest into the courtyard of his castle near Kintore, that he determined to abandon it, and, if possible, to select a locality distant from public roads, and the observation of hostile visitors. It was with this view that he fixed on the site of the present mansion; and certainly it would have been difficult to select a position where a residence became less subject to the observation of distant or passing friends or foes.

Balbithan was ornamented by plantations, and near the house, which is placed on low ground, there still are some fine old trees. It is understood that the present mansion house was erected by one of the name of Chalmer (or Chalmers, as the name is now generally spelt in Aberdeenshire), though doubtless improved by subsequent proprietors. The estate had been in the hands of this family for many generations, and was sold in or about 1690, by James Chalmer, to James Balfour, merchant in Edinburgh, who had married his sister, Bridget Chalmer. The family of Chalmer had, from the date of our earliest records, been intimately connected with this part of the country, and were owners of the estates of Thanestone, Drimmies, Disblair, and other lands in the district; and at a very early time also, the name is known in the annals of the city of Aberdeen, under the Latin form of *De Camera*. It appears that the branch of the family who held the barony of Balnacraig from about 1350 down to 1750, and the branch who held the barony of Cults, the representative of which was created a baronet in 1664, both sprang from

Ballyloughan Castle

the Balbithan or Kintore stock. Another offshoot was the family of Strichen, of which David Chalmer, Lord Ormond, the friend of Bothwell and Queen Mary, was a member; and from which also were descended Dr. George Chalmers and Dr. John Chalmers (cousins), who held the office of Principal of King's College together for the long period of eighty-three years, from 1717 to 1800. To this branch also belonged Professor James Chalmers of Marischal College, and his son, James, who, in the year 1748, encouraged, it is said, by a subsidy from government, started the *Aberdeen Journal* for the purpose of promulgating Hanoverian principles.

Since 1690 the estate has passed through many hands, having been for some time in the possession of the Forbeses of Skellater, from whom it went by entail to Benjamin Abernethy Gordon. It is now the property of the Right Hon. the Earl of Kintore.

BALQUHAIN CASTLE.

(Re-written by C. S. LESLIE, Esq., F.S.A. Scot.)

SOUTH-EAST of the church of Chapel of Garioch are the ruins of Balquhain Castle, an ancient seat of the Leslies. It probably dates from about 1340, but only fragments of the courtyard and the square tower, rebuilt 1530, remain. The first of Balquhain was George, second son of Andrew, sixth Leslie of Leslie, 1340. His grandson, Sir Andrew, having carried off the daughter of Forbes of Inveravon, was outlawed and fled to the old Pictish fort on the top of Ben-na-chie,* but was at last captured and killed by the Sheriff of Angus at Braco, where the ruins of a chapel mark the spot, and in which he was buried, 22nd January, 1420. It is said Balquhain's wife, Isabel Mortimer, threw herself between the combatants in a vain attempt to stop the carnage. This Sir Andrew had many natural children. Eleven were killed at the Battle of Harlaw, and buried where "Leslie's Cross" was afterwards erected. John Leslie, the celebrated bishop of Ross, was descended from his son by the Fair Maid of Strathavon. William, ninth baron of Balquhain, had the honour of receiving Mary Queen of Scots at his castle, 9th September, 1562. He also, as Sheriff of the county, protected the venerable Cathedral of Aberdeen

* "*Hill Forts*," by C. McLaggan, gives the best account of that on Ben-na-chie. The gifted authoress is a Lady Associate of the Society of Antiquaries of Scotland.

from the fury of the mob in 1560; for which service the Bishop and Chapter gave him a charter of the Episcopal lands and residence of Fetternear.*

We pass over the various barons of Balquhain until we come to Patrick, fourteenth baron, who did much to retrieve the estate from injuries received in those distracted days. He removed from Balquhain to Fetternear, leaving his son, George, to occupy Balquhain, and died in 1710. After the death of George in 1715, Balquhain castle was uninhabited, and gradually fell to ruins. His two sons both died unmarried:—James at Paris, 1731; and Ernest in the precincts of Holyrood, 1739, and was buried in the Balmerino vault at Restalrigg; and the Scotch branch of Balquhain came to an end.

We now revert to the Counts Leslie in Austria. Walter, third son of the third marriage of John, tenth baron of Balquhain, entered the Imperial service, and had risen to the rank of Major; when, in February, 1634, he was at Eger in the suite of Wallenstein, Duke of Friedland, whose intended treason he detected, and thereby immediately rose into Imperial notice and favour. In 1637 he received from the Emperor Ferdinand III. the castle and lordship of Neustadt-an der Mettau in Bohemia, was created Count of the Holy Roman Empire, Chamberlain, Privy Councillor, Field Marshal, Knight of the Golden Fleece,† and Governor of Sclavonia and Petrinia. By special favour the title of Count was at the same time extended to his brother and male heirs in Scotland—the barons of Balquhain becoming Counts in Austria. Count Walter married Princess Dietrichstein, and by his will left his Austrian estates to the Dietrichsteins in the event of the male line becoming extinct in Austria as well as in Scotland, which event actually occurred in February, 1802, on the death of Anthony Count Leslie, whose widow survived till 1851. In 1858 the Dietrichsteins also became extinct in the male line, when the Austrian estates of the Leslies were divided among the various heirs. Count Walter Leslie was Imperial Ambassador Extraordinary to Constantinople in 1664-5. An account of this magnificent embassy was written by Tafferner, Count Leslie's chaplain, and by Lord Henry Howard. The size and speed of the Turkish galleys is described as marvellous, some having more than two hundred oars, and doing twenty miles

* The writer would much like to know where the exact line of division ran between the former Parishes of Logy Durno and Fetternear. Balquhain seems to have been in Logy Durno, from the first barons being buried there. When Queen Mary left Balquhain Castle, on the morning of the 10th September, 1562, she stopped as she passed the Collegiate Church of Our Lady of the Garioch, and heard Mass, probably the last ever celebrated in that once fair and beautiful church. Being much interested in ancient buildings, and in their *correct* restoration, I beg to say I was astonished and delighted with what has been done at Tillyfour. It would be well if Aberdonians would condescend to take a lesson from it. Many of them have yet to learn that *mere* ornament is *not* art, especially if misplaced.

† There is a good account of Walter Leslie in "*Le Blason des Armoiries de tous les Chevaliers de l'ordre de la Toison d'or*" (p. 494), by Maurice. A la Haye, 1665. Folio.

an hour. Count Walter died in 1667, and was buried in the Leslie chapel of the Scotch Benedictine Abbey in Vienna. He was succeeded by his nephew, Count James, who was also a great military commander, especially at the siege of Vienna by the Turks, and at Esseg. Some of the Turkish trophies which he sent to Scotland are now at Fetternear. The first historical record of the family, known as the *Laurus Leslœana*, was compiled under his patronage at Gratz, 1692. Count James died 1694. He had no family by his wife, Princess Lichtenstein. He purchased two estates in Styria, Pernegg near Bruck, and Pettau near Marbourg. The latter a really magnificent feudal castle not unlike Stirling. The town of Pettau was the ancient Roman Pettovium, and contains many interesting remains. At Gratz the Leslie palace and gardens are now the Johanneum and Botanical Gardens. The family do not seem to have lived much at Neustadt in Bohemia, which is a castle not unlike Fyvie. The male line of the Leslies of Balquhain ended with Count Anthony Leslie who died in 1802, and who, *de jure*, was heir of entail of Balquhain, from which he was unjustly ousted after a vexatious law plea, merely because he was an alien and a Catholic.

We now come to the descendants of Teresa, third daughter of Count Patrick Leslie. She married Robert Duguid of Auchinhove, and their son, Patrick Leslie Duguid, succeeded as heir of entail, by law, in 1775. In any case this family would have succeeded, *de jure*, in 1802. The Duguids of Auchinhove trace a direct male line from 1400, when they first appear at Dundee; but it is not known whence they originally came, probably from France. Their armorial bearings are very simple and good—*az.*, three crosses pattée *arg.* Crest, a dove with olive branch. Motto, *Patientiâ et Spe.*

IV.

BALFLUIG.

THE Castle of Balfluig, in the parish of Alford, though it has long ceased to be the residence of a county family, remains nearly intact so far as external appearance is concerned. It is of the orthodox type of the minor Scottish castles of the sixteenth century; and the date, 1556, over the entrance door probably fixes accurately the year of its erection. Balfluig was one of the numerous possessions of the Forbeses, and the earlier history of the family will be found in Mr. Matthew Lumsden's interesting work. It would appear from the titles that a charter of the lands was granted about 1648, in favour of John Forbes of Leslie in life-rent, and John and Alexander Forbes, his sons, in fee; and subsequently, in 1650, a crown charter of resignation was obtained in favour of the said John Forbes of Leslie in life-rent, and John Forbes, his son, in fee, which contained a grant, *de novo*, of the said lands, erecting them into a barony, called the Barony of Alford. John Forbes of Leslie having died, he was succeeded by his son John Forbes, who was again succeeded by his son John. The latter married Mary Ogilvie, daughter of George, Lord Banff. In 1702 a new Crown charter of resignation was obtained, in favour of the last mentioned John Forbes, and of George Forbes, his son, containing a grant *de novo*, and erecting the lands then held by them into a barony, called the Barony of Alford. This charter appears to have been ratified by an Act of Parliament in 1705. Mr. George Forbes, previous to his succession to the estate, married in 1715 Jean Skene, eldest daughter of Alex. Skene of that ilk. He had at least two brothers, Alexander and John, and a sister Mary, who married James Gordon, minister of the parish, and for some time Professor of Divinity in King's College, Aberdeen. On George Forbes's death, he was succeeded by his son John, who made up his title in 1742. He appears to have settled as a merchant in Rotterdam, and in 1753 he sold the Barony of Alford to Francis Farquharson of Haughton, whose descendant, Robert Francis Ogilvie Farquharson of Haughton, is the present

proprietor. He succeeded to the estates on the death of his father, on 14th May, 1854.

This castle was a place of some importance in relation to the civil commotions of the sixteenth and seventeenth centuries. It overlooks the scene of the battle of Alford, and was, indeed, the only place of importance in the immediate vicinity of that important conflict. Forbes of Balfluig was on the covenanting side, and in 1662 he suffered the inconvenience of a political fine of £1800. The Scottish Acts of Parliament contain notices of John Forbes, yr., of Balfluig, as Commissioner of Supply for Aberdeenshire, in the years 1685, 1689, and 1690. In 1704, Balfluig was Lord Commissioner to the Scottish Parliament. In 1720, Balfluig left an annual sum of £2 stg., for the benefit of the parish schoolmaster; and a late incumbent, the Rev. Hugh McConnach, obtained from the easel of John Phillip, R.A. (who was at the time—1854—engaged in painting studies for his well-known picture, "Collecting of the Offering,") an excellent reproduction of a portrait of the donor, which was for a time in the parish school, and is now in the manse of Alford.

HALLFOREST.

THE ancient tower of Hallforest is situated in the parish of Kintore, and at the distance of about a mile to the westward of that royal burgh. The date of its erection is uncertain. All that remains of a once extensive building, is a rectangular structure of considerable height, containing two very lofty arched apartments, one above the other. The higher arch is surmounted by an area of some extent, filled with the superstructure which has fallen in, and from whence some shrubs are growing among the grass and weeds now in undisturbed possession of the hunting tower, according to tradition, of Robert Bruce. The castle formerly rose to the height of four stories, having battlements, besides a cape-house, with a moveable ladder by which the inmates obtained access to the first floor. Hallforest was granted by Robert Bruce to Robert de Keith, Great Marischal of Scotland, in consideration of his services at Bannockburn, or, according to others, at the battle of Inverurie.

Tradition tells an interesting anecdote of a visit, *incognito*, of James II. of Scotland to this seat of one of his courtiers, Lord George Keith. His Majesty, in the guise of a traveller, called one evening at a house in Kintore occupied by a man named Thain. After some conversation, in the course of which he had made inquiries about Hallforest and its occupants, the King asked Thain if he would carry a message to "Geordie Keith." "Geordie Keith!" exclaimed Thain, in surprise; "a better man than you would have called him Lord George Keith." Nevertheless he undertook to deliver the message, which is said to have consisted principally in the convey of a knife and fork so constructed that the handles fitted into each other, and appeared to be one, the blade and prongs being covered by a single scabbard. On receiving the symbol, Lord George asked Thain if he knew who his visitor was, and told him it was the king. The worthy burgher, bethinking himself of his conversation with the stranger, was reluctant to face him again; but being reassured and accompanied by Keith, he returned. In the meantime Thain's wife had so far recognised in her visitor a personage of more than ordinary quality, that she had ordered her best fowl to be prepared for supper, and was showing him every attention in her power. In return for this hospitality Thain received a grant from the king of a piece of land known as the Goose Croft.*

Queen Mary is said to have visited Hallforest about the time of the battle of Corrichie; and during the wars of the Covenanters it was subjected to frequent attacks.

Sir John Keith, third son of William Earl Marischal, was created Earl of Kintore in 1667; his descendant, Algernon Hawkins Thomond Keith-Falconer, the present and tenth Earl is proprietor of Hallforest and the adjoining estate.

* "Donside Guide," p. 19.

V.

BALMORAL.

BALMORAL Castle, the Highland residence of Her Majesty the Queen, occupies a magnificent situation in the centre of Upper Deeside. Embosomed in birch wood, with a background of pine-forest and mountain, the rapid and clear stream of the Dee dashing on beneath, it is difficult to picture a more wild or beautiful scene. The castle itself, its situation, and its history each demand a few words.

The castle or palace is a magnificent pile of buildings in the Scottish baronial style of architecture, erected by the late Prince Consort in 1853-56. It consists of two blocks connected by wings. At the eastern extremity is a great tower thirty five feet square, rising to a height of eighty feet and surmounted by a small circular staircase turret and three other turrets at the corners carried up other twenty feet, the entire height being thus one hundred feet from the ground. Built of dressed granite of a light grey colour, the castle has an unusually bright appearance. The north and west fronts are ornamented with various mouldings in harmony with the style of architecture, while those of the east and south are distinguished by a severe yet not inelegant simplicity. The internal arrangements are those of a well equipped modern residence, there being sufficient accommodation for about 120 persons. The furnishings of the State rooms and private apartments are throughout in admirable taste. A ball-room 68 feet long by 25 wide is the largest separate apartment. In all respects this magnificent building is worthy of the purpose for which it was erected, and it is not surprising that it should be the favourite residence of the revered and beloved Sovereign of the British Empire.

Balmoral is in the parish of Crathie, and about a mile above the Church on the opposite side of the Dee. The ground rises rapidly to the south of the castle, and the wood extends in a dense mass, or is in places feathered to a considerable height up the face of the mountain of Craig-Gowan. Overlooking the castle is the memorial cairn to the Prince Consort, bearing the inscription:—

TO THE BELOVED MEMORY

OF

ALBERT, THE GREAT AND GOOD
PRINCE CONSORT,

RAISED BY HIS BROKEN-HEARTED WIDOW,

VICTORIA R.

AUGUST 21, 1862.

> "He being made perfect in a short time fulfilled a long time:
> For his soul pleased the Lord,
> Therefore hastened He to take him
> Away from among the wicked."
>
> *Wisdom of Solomon*, iv. 13, 14.

Farther to the south-west, appears the summit of Lochnagar, which, although not the greatest in point of altitude, is by far the most picturesque in form of the heights composing the mountain chain, and is, from its associations, without doubt the most celebrated of the Grampians. The question asked by travellers is not which is the grandest mountain of the range, but which is "Byron's Hill." The sublimity of the poet's genius was cradled in the grand desolation of nature that characterises and surrounds the mountain of Lochnagar. The early impressions shadowed forth in his "Hours of Idleness," illustrative of his enthusiastic admiration of the grandest features of nature, burst forth in the course of his more matured and more popular works, and he never forgot the days, when in these wilds, "his young footsteps in infancy wandered." In a note to his poem of "The Island," he records his admiration of mountain scenery, and attributes the delight he experienced in after life, when gazing on the Alps or the Appenine, far less to them, or to classic remembrances, than to the associations connected with his boyhood and Lochnagar.

Balmoral formerly belonged to the Farquharsons, descendants of the family of Inverey, whose ancestor was Donald, the second son of Findla-Mor. The fourth son of Donald of Inverey died in the reign of James the Sixth, and was succeeded by his eldest son, William, who married, secondly, the daughter of Gordon of Abergeldie, their son, Charles, being the first laird of Balmoral. On his death the estate

Balmoral Castle

reverted to his elder brother, who married Margaret, the daughter of Leith of Overhall; and their son, who inherited Balmoral, also succeeded to the estate of Auchlossan by the death of an elder brother, and having married Jane, daughter of Mr. William Leith of Aberdeen, died leaving no family. In him ended the male line of William, eldest son of James Farquharson of Inverey.

Balmoral was next acquired by the Earl of Fife, from whose trustees it was held on lease in the second quarter of this century by the Right Hon. Sir Robert Gordon, brother of the Earl of Aberdeen. Sir Robert Gordon was in the diplomatic service and held among other appointments, that of Ambassador to the Court of Vienna. When not engaged in the service of his country he sought tranquillity in the seclusion of Upper Deeside. The small house which he found on the site of the present castle received very extensive additions from him, until it became a residence adequate to the requirements of a family of high position. The garden and pleasure grounds were also laid out with great taste, so that Balmoral became one of the most attractive seats in this part of the Highlands, except that the house itself had neither external beauty nor homogeneity of plan or structure. Sir Robert Gordon returned from Vienna in 1846, and was to take up his abode at Balmoral, but did not long survive. His death occurred in the autumn of 1847. It was on the 8th of September, 1848, that Her Majesty and suite first arrived at Balmoral, the name of which, it should be mentioned, signifies the town or dwelling of the great Earl. On three previous occasions she had visited the Highlands, and these visits had inspired her with a desire to have a permanent residence in that part of her dominions, a desire equally shared by her Royal husband, Prince Albert, who accordingly acquired the reversion of the lease of Balmoral shortly after Sir Robert Gordon's death. Hitherto, however, neither the Queen nor the Prince had actually seen their future residence. After Sir R. Gordon's death Balmoral was recommended to them as a suitable locality by the Earl of Aberdeen, and the climate of Deeside being pronounced by Sir James Clark, the Queen's physician, to be one of the driest and healthiest in Scotland, the Royal pair decided on adopting his lordship's advice. "It is a pretty little castle in the old Scottish style," wrote Her Majesty in her "Journal," on her first arrival at her Deeside residence, and the charms of the situation and scenery have always from that time onward powerfully attracted her. Some years afterwards Prince Albert entered into full possession of the property, by purchase from the Earl of Fife's Trustees. In 1852 the cairn was erected on the top of Craig-Gowan to commemorate the taking possession of the place by its Royal owners. The old castle, for which, however, the Queen had a great liking, was quite inadequate to the requirements of the Royal household, and on the 28th of September, 1853, Her Majesty laid the foundation stone of the Palace, by which it was to be replaced. Two years later, on the 7th of September, 1855, the Royal family again arrived at Balmoral. "The new house looks beautiful," wrote the Queen in her "Journal" under that date. "The tower and rooms in the connecting part are, however, only half-finished, and the offices are still incomplete." "The house is charming, the rooms delightful, the furniture, papers, everything perfection," she wrote again, "the view of the valley of the Dee, with the mountains in the background, which one never could see from the old house, is quite beautiful." When Her Majesty and her household again arrived at the new residence, at the end of August, 1856, they found the tower, offices, and everything complete; and the old castle, to which she dedicates some words of parting regret, had completely disappeared. Under date of October 13, 1856, this entry is made :—"Every year my heart becomes more fixed in this dear paradise, and so much more so, now that all has become my dearest Albert's own creation, own work, own building, own laying out as at Osborne; and his great taste and the impress of his dear hand have been stamped everywhere." Such were Her Majesty's impressions more than thirty years ago, as she herself has recorded and published them, and all through that period she has been accustomed annually to pass some months at her beautiful Highland home.

VI.

BARRA.

THE Castle of Barra is a massive and imposing pile, of which portions are of great antiquity, situated on the north-west slope of the hill of Barra. It consists of a central, or main building, and the wings at right angles with it, the whole forming three sides of a square. The central portion is evidently the oldest; and its lower rooms are vaulted and loop-holed, and form a fine example of the ancient fortified hall. Near the roof the dates 1614 and 1618 are marked, apparently to signify the time when some additions or improvements were made. The south wing is carried to the greatest height, and from the second floor upward is flanked by turrets. The north wing, which is only two storeys high, is the most modern part of the building, having been erected by the grandfather of the present proprietor.* Some ruins of outworks are still visible.

On the summit of the hill are the remains of a circular camp surrounded by three ditches, known as Comyn's Camp. The scene of the battle of Barra, in which Comyn and the Earl of Buchan were routed by King Robert Bruce, shortly after the battle of Inverurie in which he had also been victorious, is on the lower ground, between the farm-steading of North Mains of Barra and the railway; and it is just possible that Comyn may have made use of the camp, but there is reason to believe that it existed long before his time. A massive stone hammer, which is figured in Way's "Catalogue of Historical Scottish Relics" (Edinburgh 1859), and at that time in the possession of Rev. S. W. King, was dug up within this camp. Some antiquarians attribute it to the Danes.

The lands of Barra, or Barracht, belonged before the middle of the thirteenth century to the family of King, afterwards of Dudwick in Ellon. More than two centuries later, in 1476, James King, "in Barracht," and Alexander Seton, "in Meldrum," are among "the big lairds and quiet neighbours of the burgh of Inverurie."

---

* *Ferguson's Scenery and Antiquities on the line of Great North of Scotland Railway, p. 33.*

Dr. Davidson in the "Addenda" to his "Inverurie and the Earldom of Garioch," gives the following particulars:—A new charter of part of Barra was obtained by James King "of Bourtie," and Margaret Barclay (Towie), his wife, on 15th November, 1490. William King, designed, in 1506, of Bourtie and Barra, was served heir to his father in the same lands, 19th April, 1547. By his wife, Janet Gria, or Grier, he had John, who died before 1537, and James. On 21st January, 1530, John, "son and heir-apparent of William King of Bourtie," got a remission for art and part in the slaughter of Alexander Seton of Meldrum on 31st January, 1527; and for art and part in the besieging of Kildrummy. James King of Barra, who married Isobel, daughter of James Gray of Schivas, got charters from his father in 1537 and 1548. He died 9th December, 1576, leaving four sons. His successor, William King of Barra, served heir 19th April, 1577, was Baillie in Bourtie to the Abbey of Arbroath, along with John Seton. In 1583 he married Elizabeth Menzies, relict of John Lumsdaine of Clova; and in the same year his son, by his first wife, James, married Lumsdaine's daughter, Beatrice. James King of Barra succeeded his father, but sold the estate between 1595 and 1598. On 29th November, 1615, Elizabeth Seton pursued James King, "sumtyme of Barra," and others, for art and part in the slaughter of her father, Alexander Seton, fiar of Meldrum, "with schottis of hagbuttis and muscattis, committed upon the landis of Barra, between Meldrum and the Kirktown of Bourtie. In 1619 the Earls of Mar and Melrose interceded for a royal pardon to James King, pleading that divers of his kindred had been killed for that slaughter, and his hail guids had been so intromitted with that he was forced to sell his lands much under half their value.

The dates marked on the castle as already mentioned, occur in the Seton period, which terminated in 1630 with the sale of the estate to James Reid, whose family remained in possession for nearly a century and a quarter. One of his descendants in the line of inheritance, John Reid, was created a baronet of Nova Scotia in 1703; and the baronetcy of "Reid of Barra" existed till 1885, when it became extinct. The castle and estate passed, about 1753, into the possession of Mr. Ramsay, ancestor of the present proprietor.

The castle is still habitable, and in the more modern part Major Ramsay has fitted up several rooms for his own use.

Barra Castle

VII.

CORSE.

THE ruins of the Castle of Corse stand in the parish of Coull. The building has, in former times, been of considerable dimensions, and its situation is picturesque. It stands on an eminence sloping to the southward, at the foot of which runs the clear and rapid stream that subsequently passes the neighbouring stronghold of Craigievar, and is surrounded by old trees and modern thriving plantations.

The castle was erected by William Forbes, the father of Patrick, bishop of Aberdeen. His former unfortified dwelling having been plundered by Highland freebooters, Forbes vowed, "If God spare my life, I will build a house at which thieves will need to knock before they enter." The result of this determination was the strong fortalice which, in its unroofed condition, uprears itself in rugged grandeur still bidding defiance to time and storm. The date of its erection is fixed by an inscription on the lintel over the door—"W. F. 1581. E. S."—the initials being those of William Forbes and Elizabeth Strachan, his wife.

In the early part of the thirteenth century the lands of Corse were included in the extensive domains of the Durwards. A charter granted by King Alexander II. in 1234, confirmed to Colin Durward, the Lord O'Neil, possession of the lands of "Coule, Kincragy, and le Corss." A century and a half later, in 1389, this barony was resigned by Isabella, Countess of Fife, and conferred by Robert II. on his son, Robert, Duke of Albany. On the fall of Albany after the return of James I., the barony of O'Neil, with the estates attached to it, were forfeited to the crown. In 1476 they were bestowed by James III. on his armour-bearer, Patrick, third son of James, the second Lord Forbes, in acknowledgment of faithful services. This Patrick Forbes was the founder of the family of Corse, which was destined to give so many eminent men to the service of learning, religion, and their country. He was succeeded by his son, David, to whom, in 1510, a charter was granted of the lands of O'Neil-Corse, Kincragy, and Muirton, and uniting them into a "haill and free barony, to be called the Barony of O'Neil in all time coming"—the lands of Coull, however, being now disjoined from those of Corse. David married Elizabeth Panter, sister of Patrick Panter of Newmanswalls, Montrose; and was succeeded in 1554 by their son, Patrick, who married Marjorie, daughter of Lumsden of Cushnie. Patrick, in turn, was succeeded in 1568 by his eldest son, William. This William Forbes, the fourth in succession, a man possessed of much independence of character, was the first man of position in this part of the country to identify himself with the Reformation. He built the castle as already mentioned, and acquired the lands of Wester Corse and Norham, which had belonged to Hurry of Pitfichie. By his marriage with Elizabeth Strachan of Thornton, Kincardineshire, he had seven sons, namely (1) Patrick, bishop of Aberdeen; (2) William, founder of the Craigievar branch of the family; (3) John, minister of Alford, a keen Presbyterian, who was Moderator of the General Assembly at Aberdeen in 1605, declared illegal by the civil power; and who, for the tenacity with which he clung to his opinions was first imprisoned and then banished, taking refuge in the Netherlands where he officiated as pastor, first at Middleburg and then at Delft; (4) Arthur, a soldier of fortune in the Swedish service, who settled in Ireland, was created a baronet, and was the father of the first Earl of Granard; (5) Alexander; (6) James; and (7) Robert;—the last three comparatively undistinguished. There were also five daughters, all of whom were married, some into families of note.

Patrick Forbes was born at Corse in 1564. Displaying in his early days the promise realised in his maturer life, his father sent him to be educated at Stirling Grammar School under Thomas Buchanan, grandson of the poet and historian. From Stirling he went to Glasgow to study philosophy under his eminent cousin, Andrew Melville. When Melville was appointed to the Chair of Theology in St. Andrews, young Forbes accompanied him thither, continuing his studies which were afterwards pursued to some extent in England. On marrying Lucretia, daughter of Spens of Wormiston, in Fifeshire, he resided for some time at a mansion near Montrose, with which district, as we have seen, both his mother and grandmother were connected. On the death of his father, in 1598, he succeeded to the family estate, but still continued his studies in theological and other learning. It was also his custom to read and expound the scriptures at his residence. Twenty-one churches within the precincts of two presbyteries in the district, were without incumbents in those days of ecclesiastical disorganisation. Corse was one of the vacant charges, and at the request of the Bishop of Aberdeen and many of the clergy, Forbes was

Corse Castle

induced to deliver a weekly discourse in the parish church, which was situated near his castle. His action as a lay preacher was condemned by the primate, Gladstanes, archibishop of St. Andrews, who ordered him to discontinue his public teaching till he should be regularly admitted a minister of the church as then established. This order he at once obeyed, sending, however, a letter to the king in his own vindication. In this letter he stated how "the churchmen of that province" earnestly pressed him to accept some public charge in the ministry, which, "upon divers respectful considerations," he could not as then yield to; how "they next, with all instance, requested that at least for the good of others I would be content to transfer my domestic pains to a void church now joining to my house;" and how he never opened his mouth in any other part, "albeit oftener than once either seriously entreated or curiously tempted." The Archbishop's inhibition was issued in 1610. Two years later, in the forty-seventh year of his age, Forbes at last entered the ministry, and was ordained to the incumbency of Keith, from which, in 1618, he was raised to the Bishopric of Aberdeen. He was a most exemplary bishop—"in all things an apostolical man," according to the testimony of Bishop Burnet; looking closely after the spiritual interests of his diocese, visiting regularly parish by parish, and sometimes attending at services without warning, so that he might find out how, on ordinary occasions, his clergy were acquitting themselves. The Chair of Divinity in King's College was revived by him; and by means of subscriptions obtained with the co-operation of the clergy, he also procured the necessary means for instituting a Chair of Theology in Marischal College. The best men were appointed to the ecclesiastical and academic offices under his patronage, and "the Aberdeen Doctors" of his time were famous at home and abroad for ability and learning. In 1632 he was struck with paralysis, but after a time he was able to be carried on a chair to synods and sermons. He died on the 28th of March, 1635, in the Episcopal Palace of Old Aberdeen, and was buried in the cathedral, where a flat stone with a Latin inscription, in what was once Bishop Dunbar's aisle, still marks his tomb. It is now in the open air, that portion of the cathedral having been demolished. The Bishop was the author of several works in theology and ecclesiastical controversy.

Dr. John Forbes, son of Bishop Patrick Forbes and his wife, Lucretia Spens, and next in succession at Corse, was born in 1593. He studied in King's College, Aberdeen, and at Heidelberg and other foreign seats of learning. On his return to Scotland in 1619 he was appointed Professor of Divinity in King's College, and was perhaps the ablest and most learned of "the Aberdeen Doctors." It was his fortune to live in the time of the great struggle between Royalists and Covenanters. He shared in the discomfiture of the Royal party after the Glasgow Assembly of 1638. The Covenanters, recognising his weight of character, were anxious to win him over to their side, and to this end refrained from pressing summary ejection against him, though he had vigorously opposed them both by speech and pen. It is recorded in Gordon's "Scots' Affairs," how he was called before the Committee representing the Commissioners of the Covenant at Earl Marischal's house in 1640, interrogated as to his doctrine and belief, and earnestly besought to accept the Covenant, it being urged that "it would be to their great grief if they were necessitated to put him from his station on his refusal." Still refusing he was deposed in 1641, and ultimately forced into exile. Taking refuge in Holland, he busied himself in preaching, and published, besides an edition of his father's "Commentary," his own "Instructiones Historico-Theologicæ"—a work which, had he been able to finish it by the issue of the second volume, would, according to Bishop Burnet, have been "the greatest treasure of theological learning that perhaps the world has yet seen." In 1646, he was allowed to return to Scotland, and thereafter he lived in retirement at Corse until his death, which took place on the 29th of April, 1648. Some time before his death he had asked that his remains might be interred beside those of his father and wife at St. Machar's Cathedral, but this request was refused by the dominant party, and he was buried in the parish churchyard of Leochel. By his wife, Soete Roosboom, a Dutchwoman, he had nine children, only one of whom survived him—a son, "the heir of his father's property, but not of his learning and virtues." The property soon reverted to the descendants of William Forbes of Craigievar, brother of Bishop Patrick Forbes. It long remained connected with Craigievar. Sir John Forbes, the father and predecessor of the present Lord Sempill, himself a second son, had acquired it before he succeeded to the baronetcy, and on his death it passed to his second son, James Ochoncar Forbes, Esq., the present owner.

VIII.

CRAIGIEVAR.

THE ancient Castle of Craigievar is about equidistant from the rivers Dee and Don. It is finely placed on a bank sloping to the east, and terminating in a ravine, through which passes a stream, forcing its way to a junction with the Leochel burn. It is sheltered from the north and west by rising grounds covered with plantations. In its immediate vicinity, the ash and birch trees seem to be contemporaries of the stately tower they have been destined to ornament. The Castle is in the best style of Scoto-French architecture. The turrets are peculiarly elegant, the square towers lofty, one crowned by a bartizan with balustrades, the cornices of massive and noble carving. The structure is seven storeys high, and the walls are pierced with shot-holes to the rooms and turrets of the upper storey. Craigievar has for many years occupied an intermediate position as to preservation amongst the castellated residences of the county, most of which are either consigned to perfect ruin, or have been altered and adapted to the convenience and comfort of modern times. Within its walls the furniture of former centuries is still extant, and in few places in the kingdom can so accurate a comparison be drawn between the rough garniture of the baronial castles of former times and the comfort, combined with elegance, of modern decoration. The great hall, with its gigantic fire-place, its stuccoed walls, its ornamented roof, its partitions of oak, and its gallery for musicians, is a fine specimen of the banqueting apartment of an ancient baron. The narrow spiral staircases, reaching to the summit of the building, lead to numerous apartments of confined dimensions; while in others of a more spacious description, the uplifted arras forms the means of communication from one to the other. The ancient carved bedsteads and oaken cabinets, with high-backed chairs, complete the beau ideal interior of a castle of the olden time.

There was originally a paved court-yard in front, enclosing stables and offices, which was surrounded by a strong and very thick wall, with ramparts, flanked with turrets. Only one portion of this barrier now remains, and trees of considerable size, rooted in its masonry, have usurped the station formerly occupied by the defenders of the formidable stronghold.

The estate of Craigievar was in ancient times the property of the Gilchrists and Durwards. In 1457 it was conferred by a charter of James II. on Edward Mortimer, and it remained in possession of the Mortimers till 1610, when it was purchased by William, second son of William Forbes, fourth laird of Corse and Baron O'Neil. The first Forbes of Craigievar had acquired a fortune by commercial enterprises. In 1619 he became possessed of Fintray, and he also had estates in the counties of Kincardine and Forfar. A very successful man of the world, he was also a man of much consideration in his time, as is shown by the following epitaph in which he is commemorated by Dr Arthur Johnston:—

"'In obitum Gulielmi Forbesii, Craigivarrii.'

"Nobilis hic tumulum Forbesi conspicis; audi
Qui fuerint mores, ingeniumque viri.
Quad labor est aliis, vitæ dum carperet auras,
Divitias illi quærere ludus erat.
Cumque juberetur terris excedere, ridens
Terra vale, cœlo nunc potiemur, ait.
Quas possedit opes et terræ jugera nemo
Miretur, dominum plus fuit esse sui.

The Castle, commenced by the Mortimers, was completed by him in 1626. He was succeeded by his eldest son, also named William who was, by Charles I., created a Baronet of Nova Scotia in 1630. He engaged on the side of the Parliament during the civil war; was appointed a Commissioner for securing deserters in Aberdeenshire, in the year 1644; one of the Committee of Estates in 1645; a Commissioner for the sale of the estates of malignants in 1646; and Sheriff of Aberdeenshire in 1647. Sir William married the daughter of Sir Archibald Murray of Blackbarony, by whom he had Sir John, his heir, who married the daughter of Young of Auldbar, and they had a large family.

Over the great staircase of the castle is an escutcheon, on which are carved the family arms, with the date 1668, and the initials J. F., encircled by a legend "Doe - not - vaiken - sleiping - Dogs." The initials are those of "Red Sir John," the second baronet, and are, by traditional report, characteristic of the man, as also corroborative of the saying current at the time, "I'm a Craigievar man, wha daur trouble me!"

The third baronet, also Sir William, married Margaret, daughter of Hugh Rose of Kilravock; of their sons, Arthur, the sixth in seniority, succeeded to the title and estates. The second daughter, Elizabeth, married James Burnett of Monboddo, and became the mother of the celebrated and eccentric Lord Monboddo, of the Court of Session. Sir Arthur Forbes, who represented the County of Aberdeen in Parliament for several years, was twice married; first, to Christian, daughter of Provost Ross of Aberdeen, laird of Arnage; second, to Margaret Strachan of Balgall, widow of John Burnett of Elrick. By the second marriage, he had five sons and two daughters, of whom the eldest survivor, William, became his heir and successor. Sir William married Sarah, the daughter of the 12th Lord Sempill, by whom he had a large family. His eldest son, Arthur, inherited the family title and estates of Fintray and Craigievar, while the second son, John, who was in the civil service of the East India Company, became the proprietor of Corse. On the death of Sir Arthur, the three estates again became united in the person of Sir John, who married Charlotte Elizabeth, the second daughter of Lord Forbes. Sir John Forbes, residing, after his succession, constantly on his paternal estates, became a most active improver, an intelligent landlord, and valuable country gentleman, and his death, at not an advanced period of life, was sincerely regretted. His eldest son, William, followed him in the baronetcy and the estates of Craigievar and Fintray. In 1884 Sir William Forbes succeeded to the ancient barony of Sempill.

IX.

CRAIG.

THE old Castle of Craig, for centuries the property and residence of one of the most ancient branches of the family of Gordon, is situated nearly at the head of a romantic glen, in the parish of Auchindoir. All that nature, in a wild and picturesque form, required to render it enjoyable, has been added, by the growth of thriving and beautiful wood; while the mountain stream, forcing its precipitous passage through the "Den," is one of the best specimens of those gurgling and rapid torrents, which, at the same time, characterise the most interesting of Scottish scenery, and convey an idea of the force with which they roll down from their wild and mountain sources. The situation of the Castle of Craig could not have been better chosen for purposes of defence; not, however, on the grounds suggested in Dr. Arthur Johnston's poem, *Ad Gordonium Cragachindorium* where "the rocks and precipices, the caves and dens," are described as "horrible" and fitted to frighten people away, but by reason of its inaccessibility on one side. There is an impressiveness about the old square tower, some sixty feet high, although, unfortunately its turrets and bartizan were removed when the castle was repaired in the last century. It was founded in 1510 by Patrick Gordon, who fell at Flodden in 1513 while fighting under his chief, the Earl of Huntly, and was completed by William Gordon, his son and successor. Shields and armorial bearings are built into various parts of the walls. One shield, with four coats of arms, is initialed at the top P.G.: R.B., and in the base are the name Johnsleys, with initials, thus:—I.O.I.S.L.E.I.S. : V.G. : E.S. Patrick Gordon, who held a charter of Johnsleys in 1507, appears to have been identical with the first Gordon of Craig; his wife was Rachel Barclay of the family of Towie. William Gordon, his son, was married to Elizabeth Stewart of the family of Laithers. Over the old front door are the Gordon and Cheyne arms impaled, with the date and initials, $MD\overline{X}8$: V.G. : C.C., which refer to William

Craig Castle

Gordon, and his wife Clara Cheyne, by whom the church is supposed to have been erected in 1557. Two shields of more modern character are over the gateway, which was built in 1726 by Francis Gordon, one bearing the Gordon arms, with the motto *Bydand* (waiting) and the date 1667, while the other has the date 1726. A new house was added in 1832 to the castle, which then underwent important alterations.

The Gordons of Craig derived their descent from William Gordon of Tillitarmont, second son of John Gordon of Essie, called "John of Scurdarg" from his residence at that place within his lands, who, with his brother, Thomas Gordon of Rivane, are known in local tradition as "Jock and Tam." These brothers were sons of Sir John Gordon (then spelt Gordoun and Gordone) of Gordon in Berwickshire and Strathbogie in Aberdeenshire. Sir John was fourth in descent from Sir Adam Gordon, to whom, for his services to King Robert Bruce, that monarch granted the lands of Gordon in free-barony, they having been held by the four previous generations of Gordons, from their Lords superior, the Earls of March. On this Sir Adam also was bestowed by the king the Lordship of Strathbogie. Sir John, above-mentioned, appears to have been the first of his family who settled in the north, where the chief seat of the Gordons is found ever afterwards, although they retained their position also as great Border-barons down till the seventeenth century. Sir John is said, by the older genealogists to have fallen at Bannockburn; but his name is not mentioned by any of the early historians in connection with the battle, and it occurs in charters down to 1394; though he is mentioned as then deceased in 1395. He was succeeded by Sir Adam Gordon, who fell at Homildon in 1402, and whom the pedigree-writers, apparently merely from the fact that he succeeded Sir John, set down as his son. Of this there is no proof and it seems most probable, from what indirect evidence there is, that he was Sir John's brother. Sir Adam married Elizabeth Keith, and their only son, John Gordon of that ilk and Strathbogie, dying without issue, between 1406 and 1408, their daughter Elizabeth Gordon became sole heir of the great estates of the family. She married, as is well-known, Sir Alexander Seton, and was ancestress of the Earls and Marquises of Huntly, the Dukes of Gordon, and their branches; who were all called, distinctively, in the north, "the Seton Gordons."

Sir John Gordon, however, had left these two sons, before mentioned, John and Thomas, whose numerous descendants were known as "the Jock and Tam Gordons." They appear, from the evidence, to have been the offspring of a "handfasting," a custom handed down from Celtic times, being a species of temporary union only too common in Scotland between persons of the upper classes in the middle-ages. So recognised was this barbarous usage that the issue of such connections, although illegitimate legally, suffered little, if any disability in a social point of view, frequently succeeding to property, by settlement, in default of lawful issue; and generally being provided for in the same proportion as the younger lawful children of their male parent. John and Thomas Gordon were liberally endowed by their father out of his lands in Strathbogie, and became allied by marriage with powerful northern families. John Gordon married Margaret, daughter of Robert Maitland of Netherdale, Gight, and Schives (grandson of Sir Robert Mautalent or Maitland of Thirlestane) by whom, besides two daughters, he left three sons:— (1) John Gordon of Auchleuchrie, who married a daughter of Laurence, 1st Lord Saltoun of Abernethy, and is represented by Gordon of Pitlurg and Parkhill. (2) William of Tillitarmont, ancestor of Craig and many other branches of the Gordons. (3) James of Methlic, who married Canea, heiress of half that property from her father, John Harper, called in the Latin of the charters "Johannes de Citharista." Their son or grandson acquired the other half of the barony, which remains in possession of their lineal representative, the Earl of Aberdeen.

William Gordon, the second son, of "John of Scurdarg" married a daughter of Sir John Rutherford, and had two sons—William, the ancestor of the family of Lesmore, and Patrick, from whom is lineally descended the House of Craig. Patrick Gordon married Rachel, daughter of Barclay of Towie, and was killed at Flodden, fighting under the banner of Alexander, the third Earl of Huntly, who commanded the right wing of the Scottish army on that fatal day.

William, Patrick's eldest son, finished the building of the old House or Castle of Craig in 1518, and died in 1555. He was succeeded by his grandson, William, whose father, Patrick Gordon, had been killed at the battle of Pinkie in 1547. By charters from Mary, Queen of Scots, the lands of Rhynie, &c., were granted, on the forfeiture of the Earl of Huntly, to William Gordon of Craig, in 1563, and the lands of Johnsleys, &c., in 1566. In 1596 the same laird of Craig obtained by charter from the master of Elphinston, with consent of his father, the lands of Contlach and Auchinleith, parts of the Barony of Kildrummie. In 1607, John Gordon, the eldest son, succeeded on the death of his father, and became the fifth laird of Craig; he was a person distinguished for his learning and acquirements, (see Dr. Arthur Johnstone's *Parerga*), and having married Lilias, daughter of Barclay of Towie, had two sons and two daughters. He died on the 10th April, 1634, and was succeeded by John, his eldest son. The family having suffered much during the strife of parties in the reign of Charles the First, the laird retired to France, where he served in the company of gens d'armes commanded by Lord Gordon, afterwards second Marquis of Huntly; he married, during the lifetime of his father, Jane, daughter of Sir James Gordon of Lesmoir, and died in France in the year 1643, being succeeded by his only son, Francis, who was infeft in the estate of Craig in 1650. During the struggles of the civil war which preceded the death of Charles the First, considerable portions of their estates were lost to the family, particularly Johnsleys, Rhynie, Ardglennie, Drimmies, Diracroft, &c. Having been educated in France, Francis Gordon returned to Scotland, and married Elizabeth, daughter of Sir Gilbert Menzies of Pitfodels, by whom he had a son and daughter, the former of whom succeeded to the estate in 1689, becoming the eighth laird of Craig, and twentieth in direct succession from the Adam de Gordon of the reign of Malcolm the Third.

Francis Gordon of Craig joined the standard of the Stuarts in 1715. In the month of October of that year, the Earl of Mar sent a detachment consisting of two hundred infantry and a hundred horsemen, under the command of Gordon of Glenbucket, to occupy Dunfermline; but information having been given to the Duke of Argyll, he ordered a detachment of cavalry to make a rapid night march, and if possible take the Gordons unawares. Argyll's cavalry found Glenbucket at five o'clock in the morning entirely unprepared. The surprise was complete, many were killed, a rout ensued, and among the prisoners taken were Gordon of Craig, Gordon, younger of Aberdour, Gordon of Mill of Kincardine, and other gentlemen. The laird of Craig was conveyed to the castle of Stirling, where he soon after died of his wounds. He had married Agnes, eldest daughter of the second Lord Banff, by the daughter of Alexander, first Lord Halkerton, and was succeeded by Francis, his only son, who married, first, the daughter of Barclay of Towie, and widow of John Gordon of Rothiemay; secondly, Agnes, daughter of Forbes of Balfluig; thirdly, Catherine Campbell, widow of Russell of Montcoffer. By the first of these marriages he had no issue; by the second, a son, John, his heir and successor, who was born on the 13th June, 1708, and married the daughter of Patrick Reid of Haughton. Dying in 1740, he was succeeded by his eldest son, John Gordon, who married, first, in 1757, Anne, eldest daughter of James Gordon of Banchory, by whom he had three sons; John who died in' infancy, James, his successor, and Francis; and secondly, Mary, the eldest daughter of Charles Cumine of Kininmonth, by Sophia, eldest daughter of the fifteenth Lord Forbes. By the second marriage he had no family. He died in 1800, and was succeeded by James, his eldest surviving son, who married, in 1796, Anne Elizabeth, daughter of John Johnstone of Alva, in Stirlingshire. He passed many years as a distinguished Advocate at the Scottish Bar, and latterly resided constantly at the seat of his ancestors, which he greatly beautified, affording an example of the advantage to be derived, in the cultivation of wood, from a judicious application of principles founded on rational theory. Mr. Gordon, who was the twelfth Laird of Craig, died in 1852, without issue. He was succeeded by his younger brother, Francis Gordon of Kincardine (died 1859), whose daughter and heiress, Mrs. Johnstone Gordon held the property for some years. On her death in 1863, it reverted, by the will of James Gordon, to the great-grandson of his sister Barbara, and grandson of Alexander Shirrefs, advocate in Aberdeen, the present Mr. Shirrefs-Gordon of Craig.

X.

CRAIGSTON.

CRAIGSTON Castle, in the parish of King Edward, anciently Kenedar is situated in a wooded valley, through which passes a picturesque and rapid stream. It was founded in the year 1604, and completed in 1607, by John Urquhart, who, from the office of guardian, which he discharged successively to his nephew and grand nephew, both Sir Thomas Urquharts, and the chiefs of the name, is well known in the local history of the time, by the designation of "the Tutor of Cromarty."

The building, with the massive walls and vaulted roofs of the lower apartments, and the strength and solidity, so invariably characteristic of the Scottish country houses of that period, is distinguished by much florid architectural ornament. The most remarkable part is a lofty arch, which connects two wings that project from the main body of the edifice, so as to form the highest part of the castle into a compact square. Originally it was an oblong, with the two wings thrown out. The lower part of the vacant space has been, by one of the more recent proprietors, filled up with an entrance hall, which adds to the comfort and improves the symmetry of the building. The front of this lofty arch is adorned by grotesque effigies, bearing crowns or grasping warlike or musical instruments, with a richly carved pediment of red sandstone. It is to be regretted that the corner turrets, which were square, have been removed at some former period when the roof had been remodelled. The inside of the castle is remarkable for a spacious hall, now converted into a handsome drawing room, containing numerous specimens of curiously carved oak pannelling, of the same age as the building, and the remains of its original decoration. These present the effigies of a very miscellaneous assemblage of heroes, kings, cardinal virtues, and evangelists. Amongst others, one room contains the sovereigns of the Stuart family down to James the Sixth; and, in another, the carved likenesses of Prince Henry, the heir to the crown when the castle was erected, and of his brother, Prince Charles—both being represented as children. The founder of Craigston Castle appears to have been a person of note and consideration in his day. He is named, during the minority of his nephew, in the roll of chieftains and landlords annexed to the Statute of 1587, cap. 95, who were requested to give pledges or find security for the peaceable conduct and good behaviour of their respective clans; he was also chosen one of the Lords of the Articles in the Scottish Parliaments of 1600, 1606, and 1608, sitting there, in the first of these years, as Commissioner for the Sheriffdom of Cromarty, and in the others for the County of Aberdeen. It was by charters under the great seal, dated first September, 1597, and twenty-fourth November, 1600, "Johanni Urquhart,* Tutori de Cromarty, et Johannæ Abernethy ejus sponsæ," that the lands and barony of Craigfintry, now Craigston, were granted.

The Tutor of Cromarty died at Craigston on the eighth of November, 1631, in the eighty-fourth year of his age, and was buried within his own aisle in the church of King Edward. His eldest son was taken ill returning from his father's funeral, and died soon after. The castle and barony of Craigston, after some vicissitudes, are still the property of his posterity; the present proprietor, Major Pollard Urquhart, being his lineal descendant and representative, through the female line. Among the pictures in the castle, are three by Jamesone. Of these one is a portrait of General David Leslie, another, that of William Forbes, Bishop of Edinburgh, and the third, that of Sir Alexander Fraser of Philorth. There are also portraits of the last four members of the royal family of Stuart, namely, James, Prince of Wales, and his Princess, Clementina Sobieski, with their sons, the Prince Charles Edward and Henry, Cardinal de York; these, with full length pictures of the last Earl Marischal and of Captain John Urquhart of Cromarty and Craigston, are originals, and painted about the year 1735, by Francesco Trevisani, an eminent portrait painter of Rome.

* The Urquharts were hereditary Sheriffs of Cromarty, at any rate, from the time of Adam de Urchard, Sheriff in the reign of David II.; he was son of William de Urchard, and direct ancestor of Sir Thomas, who sold the barony of Cromarty, but it was repurchased by Sir John, who became heir male. His son Jonathan again sold it in 1684, and about the middle of last century the estate was for a time again recovered by a descendant of its ancient possessors. —Stodart's "Scottish Arms," p. 103.

Craigston

XI.

DRUM.

THE very ancient tower, and more modern house of Drum, is situated in the parish of Drumoak, and about ten miles from Aberdeen. Placed on an eminence, and surrounded by extensive woods, it forms a striking and picturesque object worthy of its history as a former royal residence, and more recently the baronial seat of one of the most ancient and powerful families in the county.

The more modern part of the house of Drum was remodelled in 1619, but the tower is of many centuries earlier date. It is a large and massive building, rounded at the angles, being fifty feet six inches in length, thirty-eight feet six inches wide, and seventy feet six inches high. The walls are twelve feet in thickness in the first storey above ground, and of still greater solidity in the vaults below, in one of which is a draw-well. From the first storey in the south-east corner, within the wall, ascends a stair which leads to the higher parts of the building. The different storeys are all vaulted, and the uppermost is thirty feet in height. The tower had an alcoved roof of considerable height, which is now removed, and one of less altitude and leaded has been substituted. There is a broad terrace covered with flagstones within the parapet, which is embrazured to a height affording protection to its garrison in times when defence became necessary.

"The form and construction of the tower, which forms the oldest part of the Castle of Drum, its internal arrangements, its situation and materials, as well as other circumstances, local and historical, all point to an early period, and give support to the tradition that it was erected by King William the Lion in the end of the twelfth or beginning of the thirteenth century. Its architecture is of the simplest description. The well in the dungeon, the thickness of the walls, the vaulted roofs, the windows few, small, and far from the ground, no entrance lower than the first floor, which was only reached by steps originally removable in times of danger, all show that it was built for security and defence; whilst its position, commanded on the north and west by a contiguous range of rising ground, proves that its strong walls were not intended to withstand cannon. The rounded corners of this otherwise square tower, like the round towers at the corner of the curtain walls of more extensive castles and places of defence in the olden time, afforded no salient points for the battering engines to act upon. These are all reasons why this tower may be of so early a date; and one of the arguments against its being of a later era is the useless expense from the great strength of its construction and the inconvenience from so little light being admitted; whilst, after the use of cannon, its position rendered it entirely indefensible against ordnance, which, from the adjoining eminence, might fire point-blank on the summit of the tower. The interior consists of three vaulted chambers, each of which occupies an entire storey. A small recess formed in the wall of each of the two highest compartments is the only attempt at any further separate accommodation provided in the original masonry, although it seems probable that wooden platforms, forming additional floors, were supported on the corbel-tables which project immediately beneath the spring of the arches of the two uppermost storeys. One of these floors, in fact, still remained until nearly forty years ago, when the middle storey was made into the present library. The lowest and highest compartments are still untouched as when they left the hands of the builders centuries ago."*

The Irvines trace back their genealogy to the earliest recorded ages of Scottish history; but in later times it appears authenticated that the family of Drum, the chiefs of the name, are descended from William de Irwine, the proprietor of Bonshaw in Dumfriesshire. Robert the Bruce, retreating before Edward the First, came to Bonshaw, and from thence he was accompanied by William, son to the laird. This young man became the secretary and armour-bearer of the adventurous and heroic King of Scotland, and continued with him to his death. Faithful to him in adversity, he was rewarded in his days of prosperity and of power by the gift of the lands and forest of Drum; Robert at the same time conferring upon him the arms, motto, and supporters, which he had himself borne when Earl of Carrick. The original charter from Robert the Bruce, conferring these lands on William de Irewyn, is extant. It is dated 4th October, 1324, and is reproduced in fac-simile in "The National Manuscripts of Scotland," published under the direction of the Lord Clerk Register—Part II., 1867-72.

The forest of Drum had, previous to this grant, formed part of the domains of the Crown.

The Irvines had for their feudal enemies in the north, the families of Keith and

* Ferguson's Scenery and Antiquities on Line of Great North of Scotland Railway, *p. 93.*

Doun Castle

of Forbes; while in the south they battled with the Maxwells and the Bells. Among the conflicts of the Drum family with the Keiths, tradition records one which took place on the north bank of the Dee, in the parish of Drumoak; the place is still called the "Keith Muir." In this battle the Irvines obtained the victory, and drove their enemies across the river. To check this serious feud, the States of the Kingdom interfered, and induced Alexander Irvine, the third in descent, to marry Elizabeth, the daughter of Sir Robert Keith, Knight Marischal, by Margaret Hay, daughter to Gilbert Lord Hay, the first Lord High Constable of that name. Sir Robert Keith was killed at the battle of Durham, in 1346. It appears that the laird of Drum formed this alliance more in a spirit of loyalty than from any inclination to wed the daughter of his feudal adversary.

The next event of consequence in Scottish history which marks the chivalrous bearing of the powerful barons of Drum, is the battle of Harlaw, in which Sir Alexander Irvine lost his life. In the heat of the battle, one of the most murderous on record, Hector, the chief of Maclean, recognising the Laird of Drum by the armorial bearings emblazoned on his shield, engaged him in single combat, in which both were slain. This memorable battle was fought on the eve of St. James the Apostle, the twenty-fourth of July, 1411.

Robert Irvine, the brother of Sir Alexander, having survived the battle, succeeded to the family estates, and married the betrothed of the late laird. He assumed the name of Alexander, and, in 1423, was one of the commissioners who went to London to effect the liberation of James the First of Scotland, who had long been a captive in England; he received the honour of knighthood from the Monarch in 1424. During the confusion and anarchy which followed the murder of James the First, the inhabitants of Aberdeen, relying upon the good feeling of the Drum family, requested the services of Sir Alexander for the protection of the city, and in 1440, he was, by the selection of the Burgesses, appointed Captain and Governor of the Burgh, which invested him with an authority superior to that of the chief magistrate. This situation was held by Sir Alexander for two years, and there is no instance on record of any other individual having obtained a like distinction; when the Earl of Huntly in the next century, became the chief magistrate, it was by the title of Provost.

At the accession of James the Fifth to the throne, after the fatal battle of Flodden, we find the family of Drum powerful, and supporting the reputation it had previously acquired. James conferred upon the eldest son of the then Sir Alexander, a gift of non-entry to the lands of Forglen, dated the 4th December,

1527, and purporting to be bestowed "on account of Drum, his said son, and their friends, their good and thankful service done to the King, in searching, taking, and bringing the rebels to justice." The young laird, noticed in the above, acted a distinguished part in the events which occurred in Scotland during the minority of the unfortunate Mary, and prematurely terminated his career at the battle of Pinkie, so disastrous to the aristocracy of Scotland. His son succeeded to the estates on the death of his grandfather, and married the Lady Elizabeth Keith, daughter of the Earl Marischal. Their eldest son obtained the lands in 1583, and was distinguished as a patron of learning, and for his extensive charities. He married the Lady Marion Douglas, daughter to the Earl of Buchan, who, emulating the example of her husband, in the year 1633, settled the sum of 3000 merks to endow an hospital for the widows, and aged daughters of decayed burgesses of Aberdeen. The next laird in succession, son of the benevolent couple just mentioned, was Sir Alexander, who married Magdalen, daughter of Sir John Scrimzeour of Dudhope, Constable of Dundee. This Sir Alexander was Sheriff Principal of Aberdeenshire in 1634 and in several subsequent years; he was held in high estimation by Charles the First; and a patent was made out, creating him Earl of Aberdeen, but the commencement of the civil war prevented its passing the Great Seal. The Drum family then possessed extensive estates in Aberdeenshire, and in the counties of Forfar, and Banff; among many others, Cromar, Forglen, Kelly, near Arbroath, Lonmay, Fedderet, Artamford, Auchindoir, &c. In 1639, Sir Alexander Irvine continued to retain the office of Sheriff. It was on the 2nd June, 1640, that the Covenanter, General Munro, accompanied by the Earl Marischal, marched to besiege the Castle of Drum. Spalding relates, that the laird was from home, but that his lady, with some "prettie men," were within the house, which had been previously furnished with ammunition and provisions. When the army of the Covenanters came within musket shot, they were saluted by a discharge, which killed two of their number, and induced the assailants to try the effect of a parley, previous to persevering in their efforts to reduce this strong tower by warlike means. In answer to the summons, the lady requested time for decision, and twenty-four hours were granted that she might obtain her husband's opinion; previous, however, to the expiry of this truce, the lady determined to surrender, and delivered up the keys, on condition that her soldiers should be permitted to march out, with their baggage, and that herself, her children, and women servants, should be permitted to remain, and occupy an apartment in the place. These conditions being complied with, Munro left a garrison of an officer and forty men, to live at free quarters, and enjoined the lady to send her husband to him on his arrival. He left Drum on the 5th of June, returning triumphantly to Aberdeen, where, accompanied by the Earl Marischal, he attended divine service, and returned thanks for the capture of this stronghold without greater difficulty delay, or loss. The persecution of the house of Drum did not close with this incident, for the next laird in succession was subjected to still greater hardships and dangers; he, in his father's lifetime, married the Lady Mary Gordon, fourth daughter of the Marquis of Huntly, and was a zealous friend and supporter of the great Marquis of Montrose. During all the vicissitudes of his career, Alexander Irvine adhered to his fortunes, and when the powerful influence of his father-in-law might have been supposed to control his mind, he endeavoured to bring Lord Huntly to a more steady and honourable line of conduct; but failing in his object, he joined the standard of his illustrious leader, to share with him in defence of the Crown, and participate in the dangers with which he was surrounded. So distinguished were the brothers, Alexander and Robert Irvine, that they were excommunicated, in 1644, and a price set on their heads,—18,000 merks being offered for that of the young laird. This rendered their position so perilous that they resolved to leave Scotland, and, embarking at Fraserburgh, with the intention of landing in England, they were driven by adverse gales on the coast of Caithness, and being recognized, were taken and sent to Edinburgh. Robert sunk under rigorous confinement, and expired in the apartment they had jointly occupied; the young laird, whose health had also suffered, was removed to the Castle of Edinburgh, under sentence of death, and without the slightest hope of mercy. The battle of Kilsyth saved him and others, the victorious Montrose, by a rapid march to Edinburgh, having restored to liberty many of his friends who had fallen into the hands of the Committee of Estates.

In 1646, the young laird of Drum, with a troop of horse, and Farquharson of Inverey, with two hundred infantry, beat up the quarters of the Covenanters, on Deeside, within six miles of Aberdeen, taking seventy prisoners with all their horses, baggage, and provisions.

On the restoration of Charles the Second, an offer of the Peerage, which had previously been made to his father, was renewed; but circumstanced as the family then were, from the confiscation of property and the misfortunes they had experienced in those disastrous times, added to a refusal to confirm the date of the former patent, the laird was induced to decline the honour. He died in 1687, and was buried in Drum's Aisle of the Church of St. Nicholas, in Aberdeen. By his marriage with the Lady Mary Gordon he had three sons and four daughters, the eldest son, Alexander, succeeded to the estate; he had no family, and died in the year 1695. The next in succession was Alexander Irvine of Murthill, who died in 1719, leaving a son and two daughters. He was succeeded by his son Alexander, who dying unmarried in 1735, the estate then came into possession of his uncle, John Irvine; he married Katherine, daughter of Robert Fullerton of Dudwick, and died in 1737, leaving no family, the male line of the Murthill branch becoming extinct. The succession to the family then reverted to the descendants of John Irvine of Artamford fifth son of the Alexander Irvine of Drum, who inherited the estate in 1553, and whose great-grandson, Alexander Irvine of Crimond, by the failure of heirs male in the senior branches, became Laird of Drum. In 1744, he also became heir of line, by the death, without male issue, of Irvine of Saphock. He had married, in 1698, Isabel, daughter of Thomas Thompson of Faichfield. Their eldest son died without issue, but the second, Alexander, inherited the estates of Drum and Crimond; he married, in 1751, Mary, second daughter of James Ogilvie of Auchiries, by whom he had three sons and three daughters. This Laird of Drum died in 1761, and was succeeded by his eldest son, Alexander, born in October, 1754; he married, on the 31st December, 1775, Jane, only daughter of Hugh Forbes of Schivas; they had four sons and one daughter. Alexander Forbes Irvine, the eldest of this family, was born in 1777, and became an advocate at the Scottish Bar; he succeeded, in 1807, to the estate of Schivas, as heir of entail, and, in 1816, married Margaret, daughter of James Hamilton, by whom he had three sons and two daughters. On the death of his father, he became the Laird of Drum, and afterwards reclaimed by purchase part of the adjoining property of Culter, which had formerly been a portion of the extensive and valuable estates of this very ancient family. His heir and successor, Alexander Forbes Irvine, Esq., the nineteenth laird, is Sheriff of Argyllshire, and Convener of the County of Aberdeen.

XII.

DRUMINNOR.

DRUMINNOR, an ancient seat of the Comyns, and, in the fourteenth century, the principal residence of the Lords Forbes, is situated in the parish of Kearn. It was granted by Alexander the Third to the Comyns, and was possessed by the Forbeses in 1332. A singular fact connected with the history of this family is, that the regular succession was, in two successive instances, carried forward by the birth of posthumous sons; Alexander, who defended the castle of Urquhart in 1304, against Edward the First, and was put to the sword, left a posthumous son; and his son Alexander, killed at the battle of Dupplin, in 1332, was also succeeded by a posthumous son, well known in the history of the Forbeses, as "Sir John with the black lip," who, in 1394, became Justiciary and Coroner of Aberdeenshire.

In the year 1577, the Lord Forbes made great additions to the old Castle, and it was in the hall of the more modern building—a fine structure in the baronial style—that (according to the tradition) a scene of murder took place, characteristic of the feudal hatred that had for long existed between the Gordons and the Forbeses. Many had been the encounters, and many the acts of violence and murder committed, either by the chiefs or the vassals of these noble families, resulting from the bitterness of enmity which marked their feudal rivalship. The conflicts of Tulliangus and of Craibstane, the burning of the Castle of Towie, and the still more atrocious act of setting fire to the Kirk of Kinernie, where the Forbeses were attending divine service, are but a few of the occasions on which these men were stimulated to hatred and revenge; at last, however, an amnesty was declared, the parties became engaged to consign their differences to oblivion, and to ratify this treaty of amity, a large party of the Gordons agreed to assemble at Druminnor, on a visit to the Chief of the Forbeses. Everything appeared to be arranged, and a perfect reconciliation effected. Lord Forbes presided at the feast in the hall. It was arranged that the Gordons and the Forbeses should be seated alternately, and the latter received instructions, that if all were right, hospitality should be continued to the other party, but, that in the event of the chief perceiving any indications of treachery, he would stroke his beard, on which, every Forbes was to strike his dirk into the breast of the person seated next to him. No indication of strife occurred, the clansmen seemed to have met in good fellowship, when the Forbeses, who watched the movements of their chief, saw him lift his hand to his chin, and, as they supposed, give the appointed signal; on the instant the dirks of fifteen Forbeses were buried in the breasts of their unsuspecting guests. Lord Forbes declared, it is stated, that raising his hand to his beard was inadvertent, and that he had no intention of giving the fatal signal. It is hardly possible to believe that this could have been otherwise, or, that under any circumstances so dreadful a breach of hospitality and so barbarous a murder, could have resulted from premeditated design; and it must have been his enemies who doubted his assertion on the occasion, and attributed to him the saying, that "the smoulder of the Kirk of Kinernie was never out of his nostrils till then."

Mr. Mathew Lumsden, in his MS. of 1580, relates the following anecdote of the Forbeses:—"John Forbes, called John Out-with-the-Sword, ane man of broken life, being informed against of great extortion, it came to the King's ears, who wrote to Sir Alexander Forbes of Druminnor, to put remedie therein, and if he would not, he would charge others to the same effect, and upon this writing, Sir Alexander Forbes took him at the Kirk of Forbes and struck of his head, and caused yerd him behind the church, and sett his grave about with tippet stones, wher it remains as yet to testifie the same."

In the history of the conflicts of the clans in Scotland, no instance occurs of a more sustained and inveterate hostility than that which for so many years appears to have actuated the rival families of Gordon and Forbes. Inhabiting the same district, having numerous relatives or friends warmly attached to their interests; and frequently in close contact, irrespective of the laws, and carrying fire and sword into the territories of their adversaries, the County of Aberdeen and the neighbouring shires for many years felt the effects and suffered from the devastating character of their warfare. Spalding relates, that in 1644, the Lord Forbes, with Glenkindy and other friends, fled to Kildrummie; the Lord Fraser, to Cairnbulg; Sir William Forbes of Craigievar, to that Castle; Forbes of Echt and Skene of Skene, to Skene; Sir William Forbes of Tolquhon, to Tolquhon; Forbes of Watertoun, Forbes tutor of Pitsligo, Fraser of Philorth, and Forbes of Monymusk to their respective houses,

thus retiring to their strongholds for personal safety, and to preserve their properties from plunder by the Gordons. The residences of the Aberdeenshire lairds of that time, were all less or more fortallices, capable of defence, and of these the old Castle of Druminnor was not the least formidable; its ruined walls resisted the effects of time and the elements, until removed by the proprietor, in the beginning of the nineteenth century. The part of the building erected by the Forbeses in 1577, is still habitable, and has, by judicious alteration and addition, become a spacious and handsome residence. The late proprietor died in 1841, and his estates fell by inheritance to his eldest daughter, Mrs. Grant, who is now succeeded by her son, Robert Grant, Esq., of Druminnor.

The old Parish Church of Kearn was originally a chapel built in the garden of the castle; it has been removed, and the parish annexed to that of Auchindoir.

DUNNIDEER.

THE Castle of Dunnideer, upon the summit of a conical hill, with an elevation of about six hundred feet from the bed of the rivulet at its base, is a conspicuous and picturesque object from nearly every part of the district of Garioch. That the extensive fort, and the more modern tower within its area, are extremely ancient, there can be no doubt. All is conjecture as to the history of the former, and only very vague tradition leads to a conclusion as to the date when the latter was constructed, but this is certain that the fort is prehistoric, and the tower, a mediæval work built of fragments, taken from the rampart. The fort has evidently extended over the whole flat oval summit of the cone, its form, a parallelogram, curved at one extremity, and, in length, about 170 feet by 70. From the state of the ruin, it is impossible to ascertain the dimensions of the wall; but, from existing appearances, it must have been of considerable strength. The materials are vitrified; and, lower down the hill, a line of circumvallation is distinctly marked similar to that, on a more extensive scale, upon the hill of Noth, in Strathbogie. The appearance of both is identical, and, it is probable, they were built about the same period, and formed part of a chain of forts, constructed as places of refuge and security to the inhabitants of a then barbarous country.

Fordun, and other historians, have recorded that Dunnideer was the residence of "Gregory the Great," otherwise Grig, and that he died there in 893; but whether his death was antecedent to the erection of the tower, of which a wall is now standing, or the tower comprised part of his residence, is entirely unknown. That Dunnideer must have been for many centuries an uninhabited ruin, appears to be proved by the fact, that, in more recent times, when the other castles in its neighbourhood, now also fallen into decay, are mentioned in history as the scenes of many events during the troubles and wars carried on in the North of Scotland, no notice is ever taken of the inmates of Dunnideer, which could not have been the case had it been in the occupation of proprietors during these times. It has been attempted to trace the erection of the tower to the reign of William the Lion, and ascribe it to his brother, David, Earl of Huntingdon and Garioch, but this does not appear to be authenticated.

Dr. W. F. Skene, indeed ("Celtic Scotland" i., 330), regards Grig's connection with this place as altogether a myth, "the creation of our fabulous historians," and some of the later chronicles place the scene of his death at Dundurn, on the Earn.

In a ravine, to the westward of the Castle, formerly stood the "Ward-house" of Dunnideer, erected probably for a two-fold purpose—that which its name denotes, and also as an outwork on the most assailable point, by which enemies, in those days, passing to the Garioch from the north or west, were accustomed to travel. Nothing of the masonry of this fabric now remains, but its locality is strongly marked by the fosse which had surrounded it.

The only remaining wall of the Castle of Dunnideer is composed of the strongest masonry, and is likely for ages to withstand, as it has already done for ages, the gales that assail its elevated and unsheltered position. It is from fifty to sixty feet in height, and, perforated in its centre by the opening occasioned by a large ruined window, it has a picturesque and striking effect.

For centuries Dunnideer was the property of a family named Tyrie, who were Roman Catholics and Jacobites. James Tyrie, a member of this family, had a pamphleteering controversy with John Knox on the antiquity of the Scottish Church. The Tyries whose residence was placed on the bank of the Burn of Shevack, at the southern base of the hill, held the property till 1724. It next came into the possession of the Leiths of Overhall, who were succeeded by the Gordons, in default of male issue to George Leith, the last of his family.

Although no historical information regarding Dunnideer appears to be extant, some record is preserved with reference to its "Ward-house," from which it would seem, that the latter had continued a place of strength long after the Castle had

DUNNIDEER.

ceased to be habitable. In the "History of the Gordons," it is mentioned, that, in the year 1647, young Leith of Harthill garrisoned the house of Wardhouse for the King, but was compelled to surrender it by the Parliamentary Generals, Middleton and Leslie, who appear to have visited the delinquency of its garrison by a very different mode of treatment: "the Scots in the house were set at liberty; but there were sixteen Irish taken in it, all of whom, with the Captain who commanded them, were hanged."

The Castle of "Donydoure" is marked in Hardyng's map of Scotland (1465), and is distinguished as one of the places where King Arthur held his Round Table, thus:—

*He held his household and his Rounde Table
Sometyme at Edinburgh, sometyme at Striveline,
Of kynges renowned and most honourable;
At Carlysle sumwhile, at Alcluid his citie fyne
Emong all his knightes and ladies full femenine;
And in Scotlande, at Perth and Dunbrytain
In Cornwail also, Dover and Cairelegion,
At Dunbar, Dunfrise, and St. John's Toune,
All of worthy knights moo than a legion;
At Donydoure also in Murith region,
And in many other places, both citie and toune.

* View of the Diocese of Aberdeen, *p. 554, Spalding Club Collections.*

XIII.

DUDWICK.

THE ancient manor house of Dudwick, in the parish of Ellon, which stood on one of the highest points in that district, called the Hill of Dudwick, has been so recently pulled down, that though no longer existing, it may claim a place on these pages whose object is to preserve from oblivion the gradually disappearing castellated buildings of the county.

In the 16th century Dudwick was the property of the Ogilvies, along with the adjacent estate of Birness. James Ogilvie, the possessor in 1608, had a son named John, who succeeded to the property, and afterwards mortgaged it to Lieut.-General James King, nephew of Wm. King of Barra, in the parish of Bourtie, an ancient family long resident there. In 1636 both Dudwick and Birness became the property of the above General King by purchase. This distinguished officer had commenced his career, like many others of his countrymen, in the service of Gustavus Adolphus, King of Sweden; from whom he received the honour of Knighthood in 1639. Afterwards, during the civil war in England, he held the rank of Lieut.-General in the northern army of King Charles the First, nominally as second in command under the Marquis of Newcastle, but virtually as commander-in-chief. In recognition of his services he was, in 1642, created by his sovereign, Baron Eythin (so spelled in the patent), after the river Ythan in the vicinity of his property; with limitation to the heirs male of his body. Returning to Sweden in 1644, he was created by Queen Christina, for his former services to the nation, Baron of Sanshult in the peerage of that country. In the same year a decree of forfeiture and sequestration was passed against him by the Scots' Parliament, which, though subsequently rescinded, involved him for a time in pecuniary difficulties; and Dudwick with the lands and barony of Birness were, in consequence, made over in reversion to his cousin, Lieut.-Colonel James King, second son of James King, late of Barra in Bourtie. Lord Eythin died in Stockholm in 1652, being buried there with the

highest honours; and as he left no son his titles became extinct. The bonds on Dudwick and Birness had been taken up in part by a Colonel Fullerton, and in 1650 he purchased the property of Dudwick from Colonel James King. From the former it descended, through a nephew, to the Udnys of Udny, to whom it now belongs.

The House of Dudwick was of considerable antiquity, and, though a plain and unpretending structure, was partly castellated, having in one of its angles a semi-circular tower of some strength, with a rectangular summit surmounted by a small gable, loopholes or lights being pierced at intervals on the spiral staircase. For many years previous to its destruction Dudwick had been occupied as a farm-house, but though doubtless somewhat inconvenient according to modern ideas, it is to be regretted that a building connected with the bygone history of the county should have been demolished for the mere sake of its materials. It may be mentioned in passing, as illustrating a practice of former days, that when this demolition was being carried out, the slates were found to be neatly padded and packed with "fogge" below, in a good state of preservation.* An early sketch of the old house shews a court-yard in front, enclosed by a wall having a gateway in the centre, between stone pillars crowned by balls.

The accompanying view is from a drawing taken in 1851, in water-colour, by the late Jas. Giles, R.S.A., belonging to Colonel W. R. King of Tertowie (a descendant of the above family), who also possesses a fine full-length life-size portrait† of General King, Lord Eythin, painted in the 25th year of his age, when a captain in the Swedish service.

* *Mair's Records of Parish of Ellon, p. 75.*
† *Davidson's Inverurie and Earldom of Garioch, p. 103.*

XIV.
CASTLE FRASER.

AMONG our ancient castellated-houses which are still inhabited, Castle Fraser joins with Glamis and Fyvie in forming a trio surpassing in combined grandeur and picturesque effect all other extant specimens of the Scoto-French style of architecture. It consists of an immense double square tower, flanked by a round one of proportionate size, all rising to a height of nearly one hundred feet, while two long low wings, enriched by dormer windows, and with flanking towers and turrets at the far ends, run out from the main building, parallel with each other, leaving space for a long and wide court between them. The basement in both towers is vaulted, as is also the room next above in the larger square, forming a fine and lofty hall forty feet in length, and of proportionate width. These great towers had evidently been topped by an open battlement or "bartizan;" but the upper parts were remodelled early in the seventeenth century, as was the case with many of our older mansion houses. The battlements were then taken in under a new and higher roof—dormer windows at the eaves taking their place—and the open corner-turrets were capped with "extinguisher" roofs. The date of this alteration appears on the windows as "1618." At the same time were built the low wings before mentioned, which, being of two storeys, and containing many rooms, must have added greatly to the convenience of the mansion, and to the accommodation afforded by the Lords Fraser to their friends and retainers.

The great round tower, and the larger square one, to one corner of which it joins—acting as a "flanker"—are apparently of later date than the smaller square portion to the west, which was probably built by the predecessors of the Frasers, while the new proprietors probably added, in the fifteenth or early in the sixteenth century, the larger square, and the round tower, the latter a very noble feature in this fine building. It would seem to have originally been the same height as the rest of the castle, and to have been similarly battlemented, as the rich corbelling with gurgoyles, from

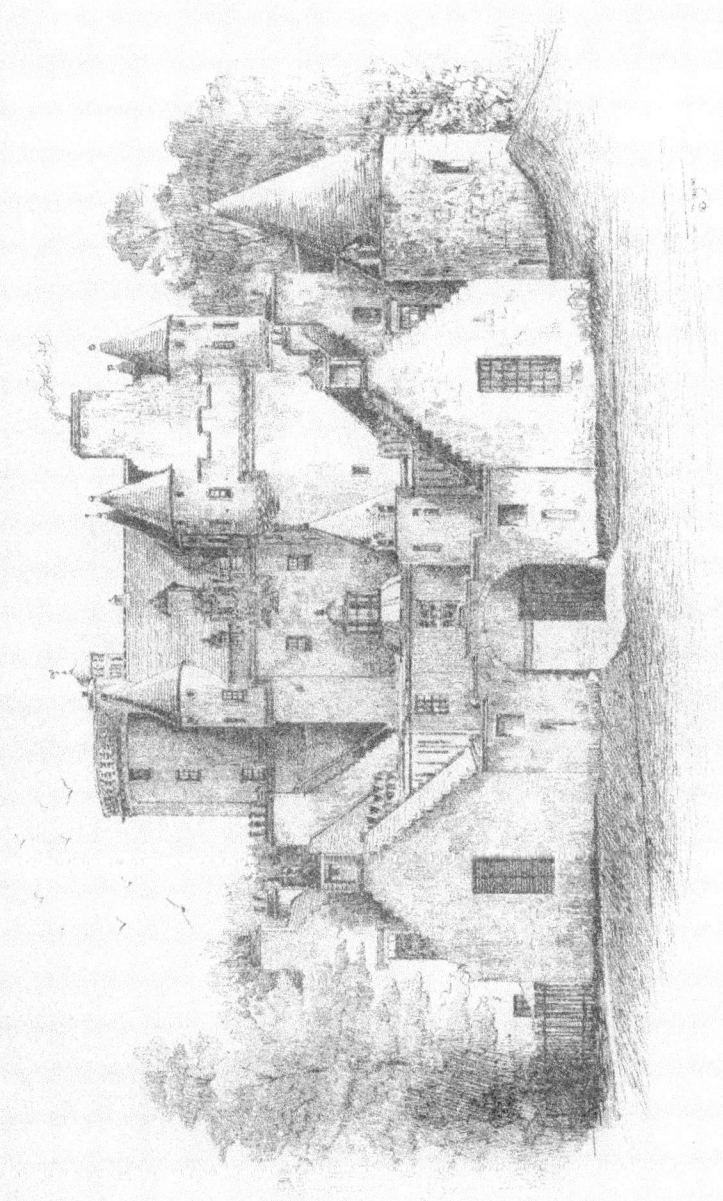

Castle Fraser

which the battlements sprang, is carried round the tower on the same level, but it has been raised at a later date some thirty feet higher, and from the remains of a second corbelling, the battlements were apparently again put on. A round turret containing a turnpike stair seems to have been also raised at the same time, and the tower, supposing the rest of the house to have remained as it was, must have very much over-topped it. In 1618, when the roof was altered and the battlement of the square towers were roofed in, those on the round tower were removed, leaving this second and higher corbelling, on which a stone balustrade, after the fashion of the time, was placed. The staircase turret appears to have also been raised and furnished with a balustrade to match. Later in the century, probably, it received the graceful pavilion roof which now covers it in.

The date 1587 appears on the south side of the larger square mass, on some fine heraldic work. This date may mark the period at which some alteration was made, not now certainly distinguishable in the building. It possibly, however, was the time at which the raising of the great round tower to its present level took place. The date 1618 also appears near these coats of arms, but placed on a clock-turret which appears to have been added at that date.

Many fine old trees still beautify the grounds round the castle, and aid in making this ancient seat of the Frasers one of our noblest Scottish residences.

The old name of Castle Fraser was Muchals, or Muchil-in-Mar. The change in its designation must have been subsequent to 1633, for in that year Alexander Fraser, still styled of Muchil, was created Lord Fraser.

The family of Fraser of Muchil was not originally of Aberdeenshire; they possessed estates in the county of Stirling, and, by charter of James the Second dated the 28th of October, 1454, exchanged the lands of Corntoun, near Stirling, their previous property, for Muchil and Stoneywood, in Aberdeenshire. During the wars of the Covenanters, in the seventeenth century, the Lords Fraser adhered to that party, and were subjected to the adverse fortunes of a civil war carried on with varied and rapid vicissitudes. On the 6th of April, 1644, Robert Irvine, of the family of Drum, took and garrisoned the place of Durris, belonging to the Lord Fraser. The Covenanters of Aberdeenshire, at this time unable to contend in the field with their opponents, took refuge in their strongholds to watch the progress of events, and Lord Fraser proceeded to Cairnbulg, then one of the residences of his family. In the same year, the Marquis of Argyll having arrived at Dunnottar to support the cause of the Covenant, Andrew Lord Fraser, left his castle, and appeared in arms as his friend and ally When the Lord Gordon was made

Lieutenant-General of the North, in 1644, the Lords Forbes, Fraser, and Crighton, declined to serve under him, nor was it until the authority was vested in the Lord Forbes, that these powerful barons were conciliated, and consented to act in support of the Committee of Estates. This incident proves the influence at the time of these families in the North of Scotland, and it must have been considerable, when, to obtain their allegiance, the Lord Gordon, then at the head of three thousand men, was insulted, and the great family to which he belonged set at defiance. The result of this difference soon became manifest; the Lords Forbes, Fraser, Crighton, and other barons, joined the Covenanters, when an assembly of their forces took place at Aberdeen. From this meeting the Lord Gordon absented himself, and soon after joined the standard of the great Marquis of Montrose. On Friday, October 18th, 1644, the place and grounds of Lord Fraser at Muchil were subjected to spoliation by Montrose, who at the time was visiting with fire and sword the estates of those proprietors friendly to the Covenant, and who had appeared in arms for its support. Lord Fraser continued a zealous supporter of the Covenant, and, in conjunction with the Earl Marischal, the Viscount Frendraught, and others, frequently visited Aberdeen, either in brief authority, or escaping from the warlike and adventurous leader of the royal forces. The title of Lord Fraser has been dormant since the death of Charles, the fourth Lord, in 1720.

The fourth Lord Fraser was succeeded in his estates by William Fraser of Inverallochy, whose mother, Marjory, the daughter of the Earl of Buchan, after his father's death, married the last Lord Fraser above mentioned. They were a Jacobite family, and their claim to the dormant peerage was never preferred.

William of Inverallochy was succeeded by his son, Charles, who lived to great age, and is still remembered in Aberdeenshire as "Old Inverallochie." His eldest son, Charles, commanded the Frasers in the Battle of Culloden, where he was killed, and buried on the field. Simon, the second son, was killed in America; and William, who succeeded to the Inverallochy estate, died without issue. Had either of these survived, he would have obtained the Lovat estates, which were entailed upon the heirs male of the Inverallochy branch, and failing them, descended to the Frasers of Strichen, the next in line.

William's sisters,—Martha, married to Colin Mackenzie of Kilcoy, and Eliza,—succeeded to his estates. The latter of whom by arrangement became possessed of Castle Fraser, and the former of Inverallochy.

Mrs. Mackenzie had two sons—Charles, who succeeded to the Ross-shire estates, and Alexander, who became a distinguished General Officer, and Colonel of the 78th Highlanders. General Mackenzie married Helen, sister of Francis Lord Seaforth, and by her had two sons, Charles, the late proprietor of Castle Fraser, and Frederick Alexander, who died in 1848, Deputy-Quarter-Master-General of the Forces in Canada. General Mackenzie died in September, 1809, having some years before added by royal licence the name of Fraser to his designation. Miss Eliza Fraser died in 1814, when the estates became again united in the person of her grand-nephew, the late Colonel Charles Fraser of Inverallochy and Castle Fraser, formerly an officer in the Coldstream Guards, who married Jane, daughter of Sir John Hay of Hayston, Baronet. Colonel Fraser represented Ross-shire in Parliament for some years. He died in 1871, and was succeeded by his son, Frederick Mackenzie Fraser, Esq., the present representative of the family.

XV.

FORMARTINE.

THE ancient and ruined Tower or "Fortalice" of Gight, is situated on the North bank of the Ythan, in the parish of Fyvie. Seated on the verge of a range of heights called "The braes of Gight," it overlooks the wide and picturesque ravine through which the Ythan passes, both sides of which are clothed with beautiful hanging woods. The bank upon which the Castle stands, is in some parts very precipitous, and, masses of rock, appearing amidst the foliage, add to the effect of the landscape.

The Castle and Estate became, about the year 1479, the property of William Gordon, the third son of the second Earl of Huntly, by a sister of the Earl of Erroll; who married Janet, daughter of Ogilvy of Boyne, and was killed at the battle of Flodden, in 1513. His eldest son, Sir George Gordon of Gight and Shivas, married the niece of the Laird of Haddo, and built the house of Formartine. Dying without issue, he was succeeded by his brother James, who married the daughter of Cheyne of Straloch, and had two sons, Alexander, who succeeded him, and William, who was drowned in the river Bogie. Alexander married the daughter of Cardinal Beaton, by whom he had one daughter, married to the Earl of Dunbar. He lost his life in a fray which took place on the shore of Dundee, in which the Master of Forbes, and the Goodman of Towie (Forbes), were concerned. It is recorded, that in the mortal strife, the Laird of Gight and the Goodman of Towie killed each other. Alexander's uncle, John Gordon of Ardmachar, married the daughter of James, the first laird of Lesmore. Their eldest son succeeded to the estate of Gight; the second was killed at Dunibrisle, in the celebrated attack made on that house by the Earl of Huntly, which terminated in the murder of the Earl of Murray. The third son was killed in battle, the fourth fell by the hand of the Master of Monteith. The fifth Laird of Gight, married the daughter of Ochterlony of Kelly, by whom he had a large family, the eldest of whom became Laird of Gight, and married the daughter of Wood of Bonnytown, near Montrose; he died in 1641,

and was succeeded by his son Sir George, seventh Laird of Gight, who married the daughter of Lord Ogilvy. Their son, also Sir George, became the eighth Laird of Gight; he married the daughter of Keith of Ludquharn, by whom he had an only daughter. This marriage produced a schism in the family and a variance with his mother. Being then the young laird, he alleged that his father had never been infeft in the lands, and that consequently he had a right to the fee of the estate. The daughter of Lord Ogilvy stoutly resisted delivering up papers in the absence of her husband. In consequence of this resolution, young Gight, with the assistance of Ludquharn, attacked his father's house, with the intention of taking forcible possession, and having lodged themselves in some of the outbuildings, for the purpose of compelling the inmates to open the gates, they fired in at the hall windows, and grievously wounded William Gordon, one of the dependents. The Earl of Airlie, on being made acquainted with these circumstances by his sister, immediately applied to the Marquis of Huntly, who agreed to act as arbiter, and for that purpose held a meeting with young Gight and his mother, which ended in an amicable arrangement. In the year 1644, the Castle of Gight was taken by the Covenanters, and garrisoned by them; the place was plundered, the furniture removed or destroyed, and the interior of the house, even to the wainscoting, torn to pieces. It was at this time that the chivalrous Laird of Haddo, after having taken measures for defence, was compelled to surrender the House of Kelly. On the arrival of the Marquis of Argyll, the Earl Marischal, the Lords Fraser and Gordon, the Master of Forbes, and other Barons, that place was summoned, accompanied by a communication that unless it were surrendered without delay no mercy would be shown to the inmates. At this critical moment Haddo's cannonier made his escape from the walls, and deserted to the enemy. The laird then held a council, and was informed by his men that they were prepared to resist, provided he could point out to them any reasonable prospect of a successful result, but otherwise they preferred accepting conditions to being forced into unconditional surrender. The laird in vain endeavoured to alter their opinions, and seeing his life in danger, repented having shut himself up under circumstances where relief was hopeless, and where protracted resistance against an army was impossible. He therefore resolved, if possible, to come to terms, and having made the signal for a parley, called to him "his young chief, the Lord Gordon," to whom he agreed to surrender, provided his own life and that of his people were secured. This the Lord Gordon could not grant. He then applied to the Earl Marischal, proposing similar conditions, which were again refused, and he was informed, that the only terms he could obtain, were, that he should surrender with his people, and be at the mercy of the Estates, as the covenanting authorities were then designated. Seeing no hope of relief, or of obtaining better terms, Haddo came forth, and delivered himself to the assembled leaders. Subsequent to these events, the Lairds of Gight and Haddo were conveyed as prisoners to Edinburgh. The latter was brought to trial under sundry charges, on which he was convicted, as was also his faithful follower, John Logie, and they suffered on the same scaffold.

The grandson of this Sir George Gordon, also Sir George, married Elizabeth Urquhart of Meldrum, by whom he had an only daughter, Mary, heiress of the estates of Gight. She married, about 1708, Alexander Davidson of Newton, in the Garioch,—by whom she had a son, Alexander, born 1710, who assumed the name of Gordon,—and died 1760. By his wife, Margaret Duff of Craigston, he had two sons, George, who succeeded to Gight, and Captain Alexander Davidson of Newton. George, the elder son, married his cousin Catherine Duff of Craigston, by whom he had an only child, Catherine, who married in 1785, the Honourable John Byron, and was mother of the poet, Lord Byron. This union was an unhappy one, and the extravagance of Captain Byron made it necessary to sell the estate of Gight, which was purchased by George, third Earl of Aberdeen, in 1787. The country-people of this neighbourhood appear to have taken much to heart the downcome of the old family. A ballad of the time begins in this foreboding strain :—

> " Whaur are ye gaun, bonny Miss Gordon,
> Whaur are ye gaun, sae bonny an' braw?
> Ye've gane an' married wi' Johnnie Byron
> That 'll sune spend the lands o' Gight awa!"

That nobleman's eldest son, Lord Haddo, who was married to a daughter of Mr. Baird of Newbyth, resided at Gight, but was unfortunately killed by a fall from his horse, in the Court-yard of the Castle, in 1791. His son George, succeeded to his grandfather, as fourth Earl, in 1801. His political career is well known. He served his country for half a century with zeal, integrity, and ability, filling the highest offices of State. He was also a Knight of the Thistle, and of the Garter, Lord-Lieutenant of Aberdeenshire, &c., &c., &c. Lord Aberdeen took much interest in the old place of Gight, and had the old Castle and grounds carefully preserved, while making the public welcome there to enjoy the beauties of the place. In this his example is followed by the present possessor, his grandson, John Campbell Gordon, seventh Earl, Lord-Lieutenant of the County, and late Viceroy of Ireland.

XVI.

FYVIE.

THE Castle of Fyvie, anciently "Fyvin," stands in the centre of the parish of the same name, occupying a commanding position on the left bank of the river Ythan. On two sides the woodclad hills recede from it; while north and south the level valley of the Ythan stretches out in long reaches of fine woodlands, through which, to the south, you see the glistening water of the picturesque lake. The castle is interesting as a noble specimen of architecture, and is mentioned in connection with various events in Scottish history.

Billings, in his "Baronial Antiquities of Scotland," says, "Its three princely towers, with their luxuriant coronet of coned turrets, sharp gables, tall roofs and chimneys, canopied dormer windows, and rude statuary, present a sky outline at once graceful, rich, and massive, and in these qualities exceeding even the far-famed Glammis. The form of the central tower is peculiar and striking. It consists in appearance of two semi-round towers, with a deep curtain between them, retired within a round arched recess of peculiar height and depth. The minor departments of the building are profusely decorated with mouldings, crockets, canopies, and statuary. The interior is in the same fine keeping with the exterior. The great stair is an architectural triumph such as few Scottish mansions can exhibit."

There are *four* princely towers in Fyvie Castle, each one bearing the family name of the proprietor by whom it was erected; and the whole building, though now forming only two sides of a square, each of which, however, is one hundred and fifty feet long, is at once suggestive of the old days of its use for defence, and its modern adaptability as the hospitable mansion of a Scottish gentleman. The date of the oldest tower—the Preston—is the end of the fourteenth century; but it is believed to be built on the base of an old tower, or keep, of earlier date. In 1296, Edward I. of England spent some time in the "Chastel of Fyuin," and the vault at the base of the Preston tower is pointed out by "tradition"—characteristically ignoring the humble, though useful, purposes to which such vaults were applied—as the king's bedchamber. In the first half of the fifteenth century, about 1440, the Meldrum tower was built, and probably a part, if not the whole, of the long range of building connecting the two, on the erection of which the so-called "traditions" respecting the castle are curiously silent. In 1596, the Seton tower, and the wing terminating in the grand staircase, were added; and the Gordon tower was raised in 1777, by the Honourable General Gordon mentioned below—who, with an amount of taste almost unique at that period, caused the architecture of his addition to harmonise with that of the old pile.

All old Scottish castles, approaching in importance to that of Fyvie, had invariably outworks for additional protection. But scarcely a trace of these remains in any instance in Aberdeenshire, at the present day, though they may be seen in fair preservation in examples in other parts of Scotland. Fyvie is no exception to the rule, so far as outer walls and towers are concerned—all having disappeared. But a square inner court, of grand proportions, was still traceable in the last century—when General Gordon made his alterations—two of its sides being represented by the noble range of building which survives. On the north side, running out from where the Gordon tower now stands, was the castle chapel, while high walls with "laigh building"—originally offices, and also stabling, probably to keep the chargers and palfreys of the family secure within the walls—completed the square. For in old days there was a mixture of homeliness with grandeur in our castles, unknown to later generations in Britain, but which may still be seen in the great chateaux of France. Under the high-pitched recess in the "Seton tower," is an archway (probably formed by Lord Dunfermline, who had built his double tower for its defence), which then ran through to the inner court, in the old fashion borrowed from France, high enough for horsemen to pass under; and defended by an inner gate of grated iron, one of the finest specimens of the kind in Scotland, from the fineness of its workmanship and unusual size—such grated defences being generally adapted to mere doorways. Having ridden through the archway, the members of a cavalcade would find themselves in this grand inner court, with the ladies of the castle looking down on them from the windows, and watching them as they dismounted at the entrance-door, which would be at the foot of the grand staircase, as was invariably the arrangement in old Scottish houses. We can well imagine that such a scene, enlivened by the rich colours and waving plumes of the dress of two or three centuries ago, would cause a pleasurable flutter among the castle's inmates, promising a welcome change from the monotony which must

have hung over country-life in an age when books were few, locomotion difficult, and opportunities for social intercourse proportionally rare.

Although the "thanage" or barony of Fermartyn was granted to different holders successively during the fourteenth century, it is not till near its close that we find a subject in possession of the royal castle and appanage of Fyvie, when it appears, about 1380, in the hands of Sir James Lindsay of Crawford. We read in Wyntoun that, some years later probably, Sir James's wife, Dame Margaret Keith, during her husband's absence, was carrying on some building; but that her workmen were interfered with by her nephew, "Robert the Keith," who, although described as "a lord off mycht, off mony landis of rycht richt," did not disdain to hinder the masons from their work; and generally "demanyt [hindered, ill-used] that lady, withyn the castel of Fivy." Dame Margaret, however, managed, although besieged, to send notice to her husband, then in Angus, of her uncomfortable position. Sir James, with four hundred horse, immediately came north, crossed "the Month" (Cairn-na-Mount), and had got as far as Bourtie in the Garioch, when Robert Keith, who had notice of his coming, met him, and a sharp skirmish ensued, in which Keith was beaten with the loss of fifty men. Having thus driven off the aggressors, Lindsay was able to relieve "that gud ladye" who, Wyntoun tells us, "led in all hir tyme gud lif."

In 1390 Sir James Lindsay resigned Fyvie and Formartine into the king's hands, who granted them to Sir Henry Preston,* son of Sir Simon of Craigmillar, in Midlothian. Sir Henry was married to Sir James's sister, but the reason of the grant is given as "for the redemption of Sir Radulp de Percy, Englishman." This is, of course, Sir Ralph, brother of Sir Henry Percy, or "Hotspur" (they having both been taken prisoner at Otterburn two years before), and in whose ransom Sir Henry Preston had acquired an interest, although he does not appear to have been the actual captor. The right to a ransom, however, was marketable, and was frequently passed from hand to hand, discounted in fact, sometimes even divided into shares. We find, so late as 1395, King Robert III. granting seven hundred merks and an annuity of twenty pounds, to Sir Malcolm Drummond, Lord of Mar, also "for the redemption of Sir Ralph Percy." Sir Henry Preston died in 1433, when the barony of Fermartyn was divided between his two co-heiresses; one of whom, the wife of Alexander

---

* The transfer to Sir Henry Preston does not seem to have been completed till 1397; and even after Sir James Lindsay's death, we find Sir Henry compounding with his (Sir James's) two co-heiresses, for unextinguished claims which they had both on Fyvie and on the barony of Fermartyn—notwithstanding that he is called in the deeds, which are still extant, "de Fermartyn," which shows that he held undoubtedly the superiorities of the lands. This was in 1403-5. The date given by Wyntoun for the episode quoted in the text is 1395, "or thereby nere," which, as Wyntoun was a contemporary, would look as if it probably did take place after 1390, when the royal grant was given.

Meldrum, carried the northern half, with the castle and town, &c., of Fyvie, to her husband; while the other, Marjory, who married Sir Alexander Forbes, brother of the first Lord Forbes, got the southern half, with the fortalice of Tolquhon—where there is also a "Preston tower"—and, settling there with her husband, founded the family of Forbes of Tolquhon.

The estate of Fyvie continued in the family of the Meldrums for about one hundred and sixty years; and as appears from the charters in the castle, some of them must have been men of superior business talent, and successful in adding largely to their territory. Their seals, attached to various deeds and charters, are in beautiful preservation; and their signatures show that they were unusually good penmen. In 1596, the Meldrum of that day sold the castle and estate to Alexander Seton, Lord Chancellor of Scotland; and under his wise, liberal, and intelligent management, the castle and estate profited immensely. Seton was created, in 1597, Lord Fyvie, in the Scottish Peerage; and in 1605, for the distinguished service he had rendered to King James VI. of Scotland when he became James I. of England, he was created Earl of Dunfermline in the Peerage of the United Kingdom. The evidence of his fine taste, and of his heraldic skill, is everywhere abundant, both outside and inside the castle, as it is, in his other fine residence, Pinkie House, near Edinburgh. The earl had the artistic instincts of his family, which were also evidenced in the beautiful mansions of Seton Palace, and Wintoun in the Lothians, built by his brother, the Earl of Wintoun. Their architect must have been a man of rare taste and genius.* It was he who harmonised the old towers with the new one then built; who roofed in the various turrets, and added the finials which prevent the extraordinary solidity of the structure from being heavy and oppressive. The huge pillar round which the grand staircase winds with easy gradient, became light and airy under his graceful guidance; and the wide sweep of the walls was contracted by the addition of coats of arms and heraldic devices inserted frequently and with great taste. The Earl of Dunfermline, among other munificent acts, gifted a silver communion cup of extreme beauty to the parish church of Fyvie; and is said to have brought to the castle many articles of great interest and value from his apartments in the Palace of Holyrood, of which he was officially

---

* There must have been a superior school of architecture in Scotland in the time of James VI. and Charles I. Unfortunately very little is known about it. Only the names of a few of the "master-masons" (as architects were, somewhat uncouthly, called) have come down to us, notably Wallace who appears to have begun, and Aytoun who finished, Heriot's Hospital. But the men who erected that noble building, and built or beautified Seton Palace, Wintoun, Pinkie, Glammis, Castle Fraser, Fyvie, Huntly, Cullen House, Innes House, and many more, were no tyros in their art; and they certainly developed a style which, although partly borrowed from the French, had a character of its own, and was, in its best examples, grand, graceful, and picturesque.

keeper. Many of these were recently, and some are still in the castle. He was Chancellor of Scotland, Lord President, and Keeper of the Privy Seal and Holyrood Palace. He died, 1622, at his seat of Pinkie. The second Earl was also a man of character and ability. He was much employed by the Presbyterian party in negotiating with the king. He was a "Covenanter" when his Castle of Fyvie was occupied by Montrose in 1644; but after the death of Charles I. he adhered to his son, and at the Restoration was made by Charles II. a Lord of Session, Keeper of the Great Seal, a Privy Councillor, &c. His eldest son died unmarried. His second, James, the fourth Earl, was principally remarkable as espousing the Stuart cause, and fighting under Dundee at the battle of Killiecrankie, and suffering the fate of many a brave Scot who "followed Prince Charlie." He had shown evidence, however, of considerable military talent, and would have been hailed by the Royalist army as a fit successor to Dundee, had not the king preferred General Cannon. He was attainted and forfeited in 1690, and died in exile at St. Germains in 1694. For the next thirty-six years, the castle and estate were once more crown property, but under the charge of the Marquis of Tweeddale, a Lord of Session, who was a relative of the Dunfermline family. By authority of the Court of Session, they were sold in 1726 to William, the second Earl of Aberdeen; and from that date till now—one hundred and sixty-one years —the castle has continued in the possession of the Gordons. This Earl of Aberdeen was three times married. The present Earl is his descendant by his first wife, whereas the Fyvie Gordons are his descendants by his third wife, Lady Anne Gordon, daughter of the second Duke of Gordon, and are thus descendants of two of the great families of Gordon.

The Earl of Aberdeen had by Lady Anne, General the Honourable William Gordon, who became laird of Fyvie; the Honourable Alexander Gordon (Lord Rockville), whose son, two grandsons, and a greatgrandson succeeded in turn to Fyvie; and other children. General Gordon succeeded to Fyvie in 1746 when a boy. He became a distinguished officer; was for many years a member of the Imperial Parliament; was colonel of the 21st Fusiliers; and a Groom of the Bedchamber to King George III. He did much for Fyvie; added the fourth tower to the castle, in perfect keeping with the rest of the building; planted large tracts of the parish with valuable timber; laid out the beautiful policies round the castle; formed the lake; encouraged agriculture; and took much interest in his tenantry. He died in 1816, and was succeeded by his son, William Gordon, who during his long proprietorship of thirty years carried on the improvements which had been begun by his father, in the same liberal and tasteful way. He died in 1847, and was *de jure* succeeded by Captain Charles Gordon, eldest son of Lord Rockville, and grandson of the second Earl of Aberdeen; but as a matter of fact, Captain Gordon passed on the succession to his eldest son, after making due provision for his other sons, Alexander, who eventually succeeded, and Captain Charles Gordon, M.P. for Berwick, who died in 1863. Mr. Gordon died in 1851. Captain William Cosmo Gordon, H.E.I.C. Artillery, who came to Fyvie in 1847, was the honoured and beloved laird till 1879—finding his greatest pleasure in improving his property, bettering the condition of his tenantry, and discharging the duties of a resident proprietor, who recognised the responsibilities as well as the privileges of his position. In 1848 he married Mary Grace, third daughter of Sir Robert Abercromby, Bart. of Birkenbog and Forglen; and, leaving no heir, was succeeded in the end of 1879 by his second brother, Captain Alexander Henry Gordon of the Indian Navy. He was laird for a little over four years, and died in Aberdeen in March, 1884. During the short time of his occupancy he manifested great interest in his property, and was recognised by all not only as a generous and liberal landlord, but as one whose benevolence was not confined to the limits of his own estate. He, truly, "did good by stealth, and blushed to find it fame." He married Catherine Jane Bradby, daughter of Admiral Douglas, R.N., and dying without issue was succeeded by his cousin, Sir Maurice Duff Gordon, the present proprietor.

The first connection of Fyvie Castle with the history of Scotland, as we have seen, is of very ancient date. In the twelfth and thirteenth centuries it was a royal hunting-seat, to which, doubtless, the kings retired for a little rest, and for the healthful excitement of the chase. It would not be an extravagance of language to describe it as the Balmoral of that day; and Edward I. of England, as mentioned, made it a halting place in his rapid journey through Scotland in 1296. The first clash of warlike weapons which we hear in the old stronghold, is during its siege by Robert de Keith, almost a century later. In the absence of Sir James de Lindsay, it was stoutly and successfully defended by Lady Lindsay, whose courage was equalled only by her fertility of resource; for she is said to have melted all the lead and pewter vessels in the castle, and to have poured the boiling liquid on the heads of the assailants. The hole—now called the murder hole—is shown through which this fatal discharge was made; and the truth of the history is embalmed by Wyntoun in his "Cronykil of Scotland." Directly, but at a great depth, below this murder hole, is what used to be the main entrance to the castle; and behind the great oaken door is one of the finest existing iron gates, or "yetts," to be found in any of the old Scottish castles; indeed it is the largest of all, except the one at Drumlanrig Castle. It measures nine feet in height, and five feet four-and-a-half inches in breadth, and was originally secured by three huge massive bolts which are still on it. After the Keith-Lindsay conflict, peace reigned at the castle, as far as we know, till 1644, when a battle took place in the grounds of Fyvie between Argyll and Montrose. The latter, after marching from Huntly, took up his headquarters in the castle, and disposed of his troops advantageously in its neighbourhood, in what is still visible and shown as Montrose's camp. Argyll, with vastly superior numbers, hastened to attack his gallant adversary; but failed to dislodge him, and was obliged to retreat after suffering great loss. On this occasion Montrose was so ill supplied with war material that he, imitating Lady Lindsay, melted the lead taken from the roof of the house, and all the leaden vessels in it, to make bullets. In 1745 the Duke of Cumberland passed through Fyvie with his army on the way to Culloden. The Countess of Aberdeen (Lady Anne Gordon) is said to have taken her son, then a mere boy, to the roadside to see the royal army pass; and to have courageously declared her loyalty to the Stuarts by stating, in answer to the duke's question as to who she was, that she was "Lord Lewis Gordon's" sister. The duke, making some little present to her son, said, pointing to the boy, "I have no doubt he will yet be a good Hanoverian." If the interview be correct, then the prediction was most amply fulfilled, as General Gordon was a great favourite at the court of George III.

The traditions and legends and ghost stories connected with Fyvie Castle are very numerous. A "Ghost" room of course exists; and the "Green Ladye" that issues thence—a fatal prophetess of immediate coming evil to the proprietor in possession—wanders in fearful loneliness through the long corridors till she disappears behind the sliding panel of the dark wainscoted room. The "secret chamber" still retains the mystery entrusted to its keeping. Whether it contains hidden treasure, or some deep dungeon for the disposal of those whose presence was hateful to the laird, or whether it is the entrance to some subterranean passage and way of escape in case the castle was taken, or whether it is tenanted by the mouldering bones of those who were left to pine and die in it, must remain a mystery till some proprietor possesses the curiosity to examine, and the courage to face the awful fate foretold by the Rhymer against the ruthless hand that would disturb its silence and solitude. Then there are other chambers reputed to have been the scenes of deeds of darkest dye; and truly in a dark winter night, when the wind is howling outside, and the slates rattle, and the timbers creak, and some sudden gust of wind extinguishes the candle, the feeling that creeps over one must be weird and eerie. Of course there is poetry connected with the castle. Who has not heard of the beautiful and pathetic ballad of "Andrew Lammie, the trumpeter of Fyvie," in which is so touchingly and simply portrayed the hard fate of "Tifty's bonnie Annie"? Her resting-place, in the "green kirkyard" of Fyvie, is marked by a handsome cross over a plain red sandstone slab, which tells that she " departit the 19 of Janvary 1673."

Fyvie Castle stands out conspicuous among all the baronial residences of Scotland, as having its interesting history and hoary tradition from a remote past, and yet having all the comforts and conveniences of a modern mansion; a place of massive strength, and yet of graceful outline; complete in the unity of design of its different aged towers, it stands now, as it has stood for centuries, the guardian of the "bonnie howe o' Fyvie."

The Staircase

XVII.

GLENBUCKET.

THE Castle of Glenbucket, formerly Glenbuiket, placed on an elevated situation, on the declivity of the hill of Ben Newe, commands an extensive view of the adjacent country, and appears to have been admirably situated for observation and defence in the warlike and troublous times that distinguished the era of its construction. It overlooks the valley of the Don, and the windings of that river for some distance to the eastward; and to the north the course of the Bucket, terminated by the hills beyond Glen Nochty.

Built upon high ground, with a rapid declivity, there are few places of strength in the county that, during times of turbulence and attack, have been more advantageously situated.

The castle was erected in 1590, and in its architecture resembles many other buildings of a similar date in Aberdeenshire. It must have been a favourable specimen of a baron's residence of that time; and the substantial masonry of its walls may continue for years to resist the dilapidation which renders it no longer habitable. The situation is striking, and although its avenue of trees has, from the road, now partially obscured the building, its ruined turrets give an interest to the scene, as observed from the narrow pass at the junction of the mountain stream of Bucket with the Don.

The Earls of Mar were formerly feudal superiors of Glenbucket, but the estate was in the seventeenth and eighteenth centuries in possession of a branch of the Gordons of Park, and were an influential family in the district. The last laird occupies a prominent place in the history of the memorable struggles of the Stuart family for the sovereignty of these kingdoms. In the year 1715, in the prime of life, he drew his sword in their cause; in 1745, bent by age, but unbroken in mind, and unshaken in resolution, he led his followers to join in the insurrection that terminated in the battle of Culloden. Old Glenbucket was one of the council of

Prince Charles Edward, when at Holyrood, after the battle of Preston, and accompanied him, at the head of his regiment, on his advance to Derby. Having subsequently shared in the disasters of Culloden, Glenbucket escaped to France, where he died at a very advanced age.

The lands having been forfeited to the Crown, the castle and estate were acquired by the Earl of Fife. They were sold a year or two ago by the present Earl. The castle has fallen into decay, but over the entrance door may still be traced, or imagined, the old family motto, "Nothing on earth remains bot [without] Fame."

XVIII.

HARTHILL.

NEAR the northern extremity of the forest of Benachie, stands the Castle of Harthill, erected in 1638. Like other buildings of a similar description and date, it has round towers, turrets, bartizans, loopholes, an arched gateway, and a moat or fosse. The walls are very massive, and, notwithstanding the tradition which attributes the destruction of the castle to fire, they stand strong and erect to the present day.

Harthill was, at an early date, a seat of the Abercrombys, one of whom, Humphry, obtained a charter of the lands from Robert Bruce, about the year 1315. He was succeeded by his son Alexander, who acquired part of the estate of Ardoyne, by charter, of David the Second. This family obtained a further accession of property, in the reign of James III., and were on the 14th August, 1484, invested in the person of Alexander Abercromby, in the lands of Pitmethen, Pitmachie, and Hatton in the Garioch. The successor of Alexander, was James Abercromby, of Ley and Birkenbog, who was also designed of Pitmethen; he married Margaret, daughter of Sir James Ogilvie, of Findlater and Deskford, and was killed at Flodden, leaving a son, who married the daughter of Barclay of Gartly; their son married Margery, daughter of William, Earl of Erroll. Two Alexanders in direct succession carried forward the family of the Abercrombys, the first of these married the daughter of James Leslie of Pitcaple; and the second, Margaret, daughter of William Leslie of Balquhain, by whom he had James of Birkenbog, and Alexander of Fetternear.

Harthill was for a short period the property of the Keiths.

Patrick Leith, the third son of Henry Leith of Barns, and fourth in the genealogy of the family of Leith Hall, was the first of Harthill, which he obtained from his father; he married Clara, daughter of John Leslie, second Baron of Wardhouse, and by charter of James the Fifth (1531), was possessed of the lands of Auchleven, Ardoyne, Buchanstown, Harlaw, &c. John, his eldest son, succeeded to the estates in the close of the reign of Mary, and lived to a great age. He wa succeeded by his eldest son, John, in favour of whose heir, Patrick, a charter wa obtained of the lands of Kirktown of Rayne and others, dated 3rd March, 1611 John, the second surviving son of the above laird, carried on the line of the family Patrick, the eldest son, was the "young Harthill" of the civil war, but never succeeded to the estate. During the troubles of the seventeenth century, several of the lairds of Harthill acted a conspicuous part, but none were more distinguished than Patrick Leith, who added to considerable ability, undaunted bravery and a spirit of unwearied enterprise. He was a firm partizan of the Government, and served in the army of Montrose. Being intrusted to raise a troop of cavalry for the king's service, he found it easy to raise the men, but not so practicable to mount them, the class of the horses then in the country being very indifferent and unserviceable, even if he had used forcible measures to obtain them, which would have been perfectly consistent with the usage of the times. His enterprising spirit, however, overcame the difficulty. Having heard that Sir John Forbes of Craigievar, a warm partizan of the Covenant, had come to Inverurie with his detachment of cavalry, he determined to surprise him; having therefore collected a body of his most enterprising friends and followers, he proceeded to Inverurie, took ten of Craigievar's troopers unawares, and, making them prisoners, he mounted his own men on their horses, and in the course of a few days joined his General, with a respectable party of Dragoons. It is related that Montrose highly applauded his ingenuity and courage on this occasion; and according to Spalding, Craigievar was "heichlie offendit." It was, however, but one of the "revenges" brought by "the whirlgig of time," for only some twelve months before, at the instance of the Covenanting Committee of Aberdeen, Craigievar had gone to Harthill—the laird being then in prison at Edinburgh—and cruelly turned the lady with her children and servants out of the house. Not long after the Inverurie exploit, young Harthill was taken prisoner by General Middleton, and beheaded at Edinburgh, on the 26th October, 1647, in the twenty-fifth year of his age. In personal appearance, he is said to have been remarkably handsome, and he suffered death with great firmness and resolution. His next brother, John, who inherited the estate (1651), was also a firm, turbulent and eccentric adherent to the royal cause. On the 24th of December, 1639, Leith entered the Provost's pew in St. Nicholas Church, Aberdeen, during the second prayer. One of the town-serjeants offered him another seat, but Leith swore "By God's wounds, I'll sit beside the Provost, and in no other place o' the kirk," emphasising the words by drawing his sword. After a struggle he was lodged in the

jail. On being brought up for examination, after the service, he vowed to the officer that he would fence the court in the devil's name. The Provost he characterised as "doittit cock and ane ass;" and, "while the clerk was reading the complaint and accusation against him, not only did Harthill violently pluck the paper furth of his hand and tear the same in pieces, but likewise took the clerk's penner and inkhorn, quhilk were lying before him on the table, and cast the same eagerlie at his face, and thairwith hurt and wounded him in two several parts, to the great effusion of his blood." The case was remanded, and pending further proceedings, Leith first attempted to burn the jail; then made a breach in the wall; and thirdly, having procured arms from some of his friends, he attacked the jailors and began to fire on the populace. To restrain his violence he was put in irons, but these soon disappeared, and on being questioned about them, he coolly replied that he "had sent them to Harthill." His next act was to let the prisoners escape, he himself "going throu the hous as ane commander, and barricading the door against intrusion." After the lapse of nine months he was removed to Edinburgh, where, on Montrose gaining the mastery, he was set at liberty.* Prison experiences had not cured him of his impetuosity and violence however, for in January, 1650, William Burnett, the minister of Oyne, complains to the Presbytery of Garioch of "the great wrong and violence offered to him by John Leith of Harthill during the time of divine service," and the same complaint had to be made again and again. Before the Presbytery itself, in September, 1651, "as divers tymes before, in ane most unchristian way, with cursing and swearing," Leith "compeared and required the silver cups mortified by his umquhile sone to the churches of Oyne and Rayne"—the ministers being ordered to bring the cups to the Presbytery, that they may be "disposed upon;" and in the following April he appeared again before the Presbytery and "in ane most blasphemous and barbarous way, with cursing and imprecations did threaten dyvers brethren, and did break the windows."† There can be little doubt the laird was scarcely answerable for his actions. This, however, does not seem to have occurred to his contemporaries.

John Leith was succeeded by his son, William, who married the eldest daughter of the seventh baron of Pitcaple; to him followed three lairds of the name of Patrick, in regular succession, from father to son. The last of the three is said to have quarrelled with his neighbours, set fire to the castle, and left the country. The estate and the ruined tower thereupon passed to the Erskines of Pittodrie.

* Davidson—"Inverurie and the Earldom of the Garioch," *p. 252.*
† *id., pp. 305, 309, 310.*

The account given by Spalding of the method taken by the laird of Harthill, in 1645, to recover a friend and kinsman, made prisoner by the laird of Craigievar, is characteristic of the state of society in those days:—" Aluaies—Leith of Harthill, cam fra the Camp to the Gareoche, with sum soldiouris, and heiring that Craigiewar had maisterfullie taken George Gordoun of Rynnie, [at his] owne hand, he takis Johne and Mr. Alexander Farqu[hars, cu]singes to Craigiewar, and keipis them fast in Harthill, whill the said George Gordoun wes set to libertie.—Harthill burnes the toun and landis of Thombeg, occupeit be Williame Forbes, bot pertening in heritage to the Laird of Monymusk, becaus the said Williame Forbes had plunderit from his servand sum moneyis with his baggage hors; theirefter mans and fortefeis his awin hous of Harthill, for his awin defens." " Ye heard befor how Harthill had brynt Thombeg, and taken the Farquhars, whom he took to releive George Gordon of Reynnie, that Craigiewar had takin befor, wherupon he and the Farquhars were set to libertie; Harthill forsees, and mans his hous, a stronghold. The Forbesses and Frasers gathers against him, but did no hurt."

XIX.

HUNTLY.

THE Castle of Huntly, anciently called Strathbolgyn and Strathbolgie, stands on an eminence overhanging the river Deveron, about a quarter of a mile from its confluence with the Bogie, and in the angle between them. It is about the same distance from the village of Huntly, which, in the middle ages, went by the name of "The Raws (rows of houses) o' Strathbogie."

The name of Huntly only became attached to the castle in 1505-6, when the third Earl of Huntly obtained from King James IV. a fresh charter to himself and his heirs of the lands and baronies of Strathbolgie, Tough, Cluny, Aboyne, Glentanyr, and Glenmuick,—incorporating the same into "a free barony and earldom, to be called the barony and earldom of Huntly,—and the principal messuage of the same, which formerly was called Strathbolgie, to be called the Castle of Huntly in all time to come." The name was taken, it need scarcely be said, from the ancient territory of Huntly, in Berwickshire, which the Gordons had possessed from the twelfth century.

Strathbogie, when first mentioned in record, appears among the possessions of Duncan, Earl of Fife, who died in 1203. He conveyed it to his third son, David, whose grandson, John of Strathbogie (David and his descendants having assumed their surname from the lands), married Ada, Countess of Atholl, who brought that earldom to her husband. Their great-grandson, David Strathbogie, Earl of Atholl, after supporting Robert Bruce in his days of adversity, turned against the king at an unfortunate moment for himself, as it was shortly before Bannockburn, King Robert's final and conclusive success. The earl was forfeited in his great estates, which the king bestowed on his supporters, the lordship of Strathbogie being granted to Sir Adam Gordon of that ilk and Huntly, who, curiously enough had only lately come over to the royal party, having till then followed his feudal superior, the Earl of March, who was in the English interest. The son and grandson of Sir Adam

Gordon received confirmatory grants from the crown, but the Earls of Atholl having returned to a wavering allegiance, during the fourteenth century, it was not till their disappearance in the person of the thirteenth earl—who died in England, leaving two daughters only—that the Gordons appear to have obtained absolute possession of these lands. In 1376, King Robert II. grants to Sir John Gordon the barony of Strathbogie, confirming the grant made by King Robert I. "to his great-grandfather, Sir Adam Gordon." Sir John, accordingly, was the first of the family whose name appears in our northern records. He is mentioned in Aberdeenshire charters in 1391, and seems to have died in or shortly before 1395, though erroneously said by the genealogists to have been killed at Otterburn in 1388. His collateral descendant, Elizabeth Gordon, heiress, on the death of her brother, John, to her father, Sir Adam Gordon, killed at Homildon in 1402, married, in or before 1408, Sir Alexander Seton, and, from her, as is well known, descended the great Earls and Marquises of Huntly, afterwards Dukes of Gordon, and several branches, some bearing the name of Gordon, others of Seton, the former being known in local history as the Seton-Gordons.

The castle of Huntly, as it now is, gives but an imperfect idea of what its former grandeur must have been. But a careful examination of what remains, and of what notices are extant as to its vicissitudes, enable us, to a certain extent, to understand its plan and history. No record of the building exists prior to the sixteenth century, but the mason work, in some degree, tells its own tale.

The principal feature of the castle appears to have been the great square tower which still exists, having a round tower at its south-west corner of proportionate bulk. These, with a range of building running eastwards, much lower than the tower, although three stories high, formed the south side of a great inner court; the east and north sides of which were continued by other buildings, now greatly ruined, but showing that their lower story had been vaulted. Through the centre of this east side was the archway, or barbican, leading into the courtyard; and here there are still considerable indications of strong outer defences, including a dry moat, over which a drawbridge would lead to the entrance. The fourth or west side of the inner court appears to have latterly been closed in by a wall only; but outside of it is a circular mound which looks as if it had been to some extent artificially shaped. It bears some resemblance, though on a smaller scale, to "the Bass," on which it is now believed the castle of Inverurie originally stood. It is not unlikely that the first stronghold of the Strathbolgie family was raised, in part at least, on this mound, being probably only a stockade, formed of trunks of trees, till stone and lime could

be brought into use to erect a more durable and defensible fortalice. In a drawing of the old castle, dated 1779, a ruined building is shown, apparently a flanking tower at the north-west corner of the great courtyard, and the north-east corner was probably furnished with the same defence.

The most ancient part of the building is evidently the lower portion of the great square and round towers. There are two tier of vaults, which, from the thickness of their walls and unusual shape of the doorways—the lintels of which are straight in the centre, but sloping downwards at the ends—appear to be of considerable antiquity, dating, possibly, from the time of the Strathbolgies. The massive pile which towers above was raised, there can be no doubt, at different periods by the Gordons. In the base of the round tower is what was manifestly the "massy-more," or dungeon, which is entered by a door placed eight feet above its floor, to reach which, outside, one ascends several steps at the end of a vaulted passage. The entrance to the castle itself is in the court, at the foot of a spacious round tower, in which was the great staircase, now ruined; and which was topped by a square "capehouse," all apparently somewhat later in date than the great square and round towers, and probably built in the sixteenth century, when George, fourth Earl of Huntly, who afterwards fell at Corrichie, appears to have added largely to the splendour of his residence. Our great historical antiquarian, the late Joseph Robertson, LL.D., tells us, when speaking of the expedition to the north of Mary Queen of Scots and her brother, the Earl of Murray ("*Inventories of Mary Queen of Scots,*" *Preface, p.* xxiv.)— "It must not be supposed that Scotland could show many castles like Strathbogie. The pile had been newly enlarged and adorned in such a way, it is said, as to move the envy of the queen-regent [Mary of Guise] and her French retinue, whom it received as guests in 1556. More recently the English envoy to the court of Holyrood, who spent two nights within its walls, described it as 'a fair house, the best furnished he had seen since he passed the Tweed, and of marvellous great cheer.' Buchanan speaks of the earl as by far the wealthiest noble in the land. Knox tells how he was reputed the wisest, the richest, and the most powerful man in Scotland; and adds that, in the world's estimation, the realm had not, for three hundred years, produced such another under the degree of a prince."

This great magnate, of whom Scotland might have been proud, was, unhappily for himself, of the unpopular religion; and being goaded by the machinations of Murray into rising against the crown, was defeated and slain at Corrichie in 1562. Strathbogie was wrecked and pillaged, probably by orders of the Earl of Murray, under whose guidance the young queen made the expedition to the north, which resulted in the ruin of the Gordons, and the death of the earl and of his eldest son, Sir John Gordon. Mary's household-books show how valuable were the spoils of Strathbogie that were sent to Holyrood, while her brother was not above using part of the rich furnishings of Huntly's mansion to fit up the castle of Darnaway in his newly acquired territory of Murray-land. But though the chroniclers tell us that the castle of Strathbogie was then wholly destroyed, they must have alluded principally to the fortifications, as there remains at the present day the earlier date, 1553, plainly visible on a stone which acted as finial to a gable at the west end of the highest part of the great square tower.

George, fifth Earl of Huntly, who was eventually re-installed by Queen Mary in his title and lands, was second son of the Corrichie earl. He must have repaired the injury done to Strathbogie, as it continued to be the principal stronghold of the family. He died in 1576, and was succeeded by his eldest son (by his wife, a daughter of the Duke of Chatelherault), George, Master of Huntly, who became sixth earl, and seems to have been a striking example of the grandeur of position enjoyed by the head of the great family of Gordon. His territories and jurisdiction stretched from the east to the western sea; he was a favourite with his sovereign, King James VI.; and but for difficulties arising from his adhering to the old family faith, his life might have gone smoothly. As it was, however, he joined with the other "Popish lords" in the insurrection which led to the battle of Glenlivet or Balrinnes. In this obstinate fight the Earls of Erroll and Huntly, with only from twelve to fifteen hundred men—mostly well mounted and armed however, being gentlemen of Aberdeen and Banffshires, with their followers—drove back Argyll and his Highland army, estimated at from seven to ten thousand, being, however, a good deal assisted by the use of two fieldpieces they had with them, and by the dread of cavalry always felt by the Highlanders.

But although "the lords" had gained the field, they could do little more, for their loss was serious. Erroll, whose spirit and valour were conspicuous, was sorely wounded in the thigh and arm. Sir Patrick Gordon of Auchindoun, Huntly's uncle, "an expert and courageous captain," was killed. Also, although not many of their little army had fallen, many were wounded; and, as we are told by the Rev. James Melville, "their horses all spoilld . . . quihilk made tham unable thereftr to mak anie resistance to the king's armie." The rebellion, in fact, collapsed. Huntly on the king's approach went into Sutherland,—where his kinsman, the earl, received him,—for James VI., pacific as he was, had been persuaded to come in person to chastise the rebels. This, it is asserted, was against his inclination, as he had, it is believed, a favour for the lords; but clerical authority was too powerful, and he submitted. He was accompanied, among others, by Mr. James Melville, above mentioned, and his uncle, "Mr. Andro," who appear to have favoured harsh measures. When it was proposed to spare Strathbogie, to which the king and the majority of the council inclined, Mr. James tells us, exultingly, that "my uncle, Mr. Andro, . . . reasoned and bure out the mater sa, be the assistance of the guid Lord Lindsay [&c., &c.], that at last the king takes upon him, contrair to the graitest part of the counsall to conclude the demolishing of the hous, and giff command to the maister of wark to that effect, quhilk was not long in executing by the souldiers." Sir Robert Gordon of Gordonstoun says that "the pretence and cullor for casting down these houses [Slains had been destroyed shortly before] was becaus that in them ware harboured priests and Jesuits." In this case, as before, it can only have been the fortifications that were "cassen doun," as mediæval mortar became as hard as the stone, and it would have taken the "souldiers" many weeks and many barrels of gunpowder to really destroy so great a pile. Besides, the fact that the king remained ten days at Strathbogie, and the date which survives, of forty-one years earlier, precluded very great destruction. Huntly, having made his submission to the king, was pardoned two years afterwards, was restored to his honours in 1597, and created Marquis of Huntly in 1599.

Sir Robert Gordon, who seems to have loved and admired his kinsman, records:—"Thus the Marquis of Huntlie, haveing fortunatelie red himself out of his great trouble, resolved to leave [live] at home frie from factions and vexations of the court. He gave himself whollie to policie, planting and building. He repaired Strathbogie to his great coast and charges, after it had been demolished and throwen down. He built a house at Keankaill or Hunthall, on Dee, called the New hous [Dee Castle], which standeth in the midst of thrie hunting forests of his own. He built the house of Riffen [Ruthven] in Badenoch tuyse, being burnt by adventure and negligence of his servants, after he had once finished the same. He built a new hous in Aboyn; he repaired his hous in Elgyn; he hath built a hous in the Plewlands in Murray [Gordonstoun]; he hath inlarged and decored the hous of Boig-Gight [Gordon Castle], which he hath parked about. He repaired his hous in the Old Town of Aberdeen," &c., &c.

The time when the Marquis of Huntly turned his attention to "policie" and architecture was a favourable one. A taste for greater comfort and beauty in our dwellings was awakening, as the country became less disturbed by "feudal jars," and, wherever they sprang from, competent architects, men of culture and skill, were there to supply the demand.

Certainly the way in which they dealt with Strathbogie was a credit to Scottish art. The upper portion of the south front is, even in ruin and mutilated as we see it, one of the most charming of the architectural relics left to us. The row of oriel windows, a feature unique in Scotland, with which the "master builder" has replaced the grim battlements of previous centuries, are singularly happy in design, and give a lightness and grace to the upper part of the stern old pile which they crown, most satisfactory to the beholder. Their material, a warm coloured freestone, adds to the effect. On two bands of the same stone, which border the oriels above and below, were the inscriptions, now slightly mutilated at the end :—

    GEORGE . GORDOVN . FIRST . MARQVIS . OF . HVNTLIE . 16 .
    HENRIETTE . STEVART . MARQVISSE . OF . HVNTLIE . 02 .

Another very beautiful oriel, though different in design, was thrown out from the upper part of the great round tower, immediately under a fine bold cornice, from which the parapet of the bartizan, or battlement, had formerly sprung. These windows are conjectured to have been copied from some similar ones in the palace of Blois, seen by the marquis when commanding the Scottish Archer Guard in France. They certainly are like, but those at Huntly, although smaller, are more beautiful.

The entrance door to the castle, at the bottom of the tower in the courtyard, was also finely decorated at the same period, being enriched with sacred and heraldic designs. As was customary, the marquis, being a crown-vassal, gave the principal place over the door-way to the royal arms,—which are impaled with those of Denmark, with two thistles and a jewel, like that of St. Andrew, at foot. The supporters are, dexter, the unicorn for Scotland, sinister, the dragon for Denmark. Above is the crown, with the lion sejant, and the motto "In defens." On either side are inscribed J. R. 6 (Jacobus Rex 6), and A. R. S. (Anna Regina Sua). Above the royal arms is a square panel in stone from which, as probably savouring of "Papistry," the subject has been chiselled off, as it has from that immediately over it, though there a crucifixion can be dimly discerned. Over all was a figure of St. Michael triumphing over the dragon,* also nearly obliterated, as is said, by a parliamentary officer in the civil war. Under the royal escutcheon are the arms of the marquis, impaled with those of the marchioness, a daughter of Esme, Duke of Lennox, with his crest and supporters, surmounted by the mottoes of the two families, "Bydand," (biding, or waiting) and "Avant Dernlie."

---

* The marquis's father was a knight of the French order of St. Michael, these religious emblems may have been placed there by him.

HUNTLY.

Nor was the interior of the castle neglected. Even towards the close of the last century vestiges of its decorations remained, as may be gathered from the old Statistical Account written about 1790.

"Nigh to the Bridge of Doveron stand the remains of Huntly Castle, which still afford a striking proof of the grandeur and hospitality of that ancient family. . . . . . A spacious turnpike stair leads to what has been a very grand hall, and still bears the marks of splendour and magnificence. Its length is about forty-three feet, its breadth twenty-nine, and its height sixteen. There is another grand apartment immediately over this, thirty-seven feet in length and twenty-nine in breadth. The chimneys of both are highly ornamented with curious sculpture of various figures, which, considering the inattention paid to this once magnificent fabric, are still in a tolerable state of preservation, . . . indeed most of the apartments are still so, particularly the ceilings, which are ornamented with a great variety of paintings in small divisions, containing many emblematical figures, with verses expressive of some moral sentiment in doggerel rhime. On the avenue which leads to the castle there are two square towers which had defended the gateway, and which the writer has seen adorned with the arms of the family, cut out in stone, in the front of the wall adjoining each tower, in good repair. The hewn stone of the windows and corners has been taken out, and applied to ignoble purposes." This account shews that the castle remained then in much the same state as when Cordiner described it a dozen years earlier. He says, "Great part of the castle seems to be very old, and is nearly demolished, but there is a massy building of a more modern date (?) in which some of the apartments, and in particular the curious ceilings, are pretty entire. They are painted with a great variety of subjects, in small divisions, a few lines of poetry underneath each describe the subject of the piece. In the chamber which was appointed for a chapel, the parables and other sacred subjects are represented in the same style."

One of the chimney-pieces above mentioned still remains,—a beautiful piece of sculpture in the same warm-coloured freestone. Although it has been the subject of deliberate mutilation in some of its features, notably two figures in armour that stand one on each side of the fire-place, and, the castle being roofless, everything is exposed to the winter's frost, it is yet in marvellous preservation. It is a fine piece of heraldic work, admirably cut, giving again the royal and the family arms, with the names, monogram, and coronet of the marquis and his wife, and the date 1606. There are also two mottoes intermixed with the sculpture. One in an oval round the monogram runs,—

"Sen . God . doth . us . defend .
Ve . sal . prevail . unto . the . end,"—

the other running across above the fire-place, reads,—

"To . thaes . that . love . God . al . thinges . virkis . to . the . best."

These might have disarmed even Mr. Andro Melville, had they existed in his era! The other chimney-piece, in what had been the great hall, is not so elaborate, but has the family arms sculptured on it, between two medallions, in which are bust portraits of the marquis and marchioness in low relief.

After the death of the first Marquis of Huntly, in 1636, Strathbogie, although it continued to be the great stronghold of the family and its refuge in troublous times, seems to have become partly deserted in favour of the "Bog o' Gight," now Gordon Castle. The latter, from all accounts, had more of the manor house character, and, enjoying a more genial climate and richer soil, would, no doubt, seem more attractive as a residence, especially after it had been "inlarged and parked about" by the first marquis. The proud title of the Huntlys had been the "Cock of the North," and now was jestingly added that of "Goodman of the Bog."

George, second marquis of Huntly, led a troubled life. Passionately loyal to his sovereign, he supported Charles I. devotedly and blindly. But he never could heartily join with Montrose in his efforts on behalf of the crown, and the royal cause suffered in consequence. The marquis, in fact, never thoroughly trusted Montrose. He could not forget that the brilliant cavalier, who beat the forces of the Scottish Parliament wherever he found them, had been an equally fervid Covenanter, nor, it may be, could he forget, even if he forgave, the fact that, in that character, he had dragged him, the King's faithful servant, a prisoner to Edinburgh. This irresolution, together with his great power in the north,—which in the hands of an "unfriend" was a danger to the Estates,—his religion, his whole position were all against Huntly, and he died on the scaffold, true to his own loyal words, "You may take my head from my shoulders, but not my heart from my king."

The marquis's eldest son, George, Lord Gordon, fell at the battle of Alford, in 1645, unmarried; the second, James, Viscount Aboyne, escaped to France after Philiphaugh, and died, also unmarried, at Paris in 1649, of grief it is said at the death of Charles I.

Lord Lewis, the third son, succeeded as third marquis; the fourth, Lord Charles, was created Earl of Aboyne, and was ancestor of the present Marquis of Huntly. The fifth son, Lord Henry, was in the service of the king of Poland, but eventually died at Strathbogie. The pretended forfeiture of the Huntly title and estates was rescinded by Charles II. in 1651, and the third marquis died in 1653, leaving by

Fireplace Huntly Castle

his wife, Isabella Grant of Grant, a son, George, fourth Marquis of Huntly, and first Duke of Gordon, so created by Charles II. in 1684. His Grace had seen much military service on the Continent under the great Turenne, and in the army of the Prince of Orange, but he held out the castle of Edinburgh against the latter for King James, in 1689, until, his provisions failing, he made an honourable convention by which he marched out with the honours of war. He afterwards submitted to King William, but, probably from being a Roman Catholic, he appears to have been constantly harassed, down to his death in 1716, by suspicions of disloyalty entertained by the government, while at the same time, he was coldly looked upon by the Jacobites.

By his wife, Lady Elizabeth Howard, daughter of the Duke of Norfolk, he left a son, Alexander, second duke, who, as Marquis of Huntly, was "out" in the rebellion of 1715, commanding a large body of Gordon cavalry, and fought at Sheriffmuir. He afterwards made his peace with government, and died in 1728. He had married Lady Henrietta Mordaunt, daughter of the celebrated Earl of Peterborough, by whom he had several sons, first, Cosmo, who succeeded him; second, Lord Lewis, of Jacobite memory, whose name is embalmed in the beautiful song, "Oh send Lewie Gordon hame," and who died, unmarried, at Montreuil, in 1754, a colonel in the French service; third, Lord Adam, a general in the British army, who died in 1801.

Cosmo, third duke, K.T., married Lady Catherine Gordon, daughter of his brother-in-law, the second Earl of Aberdeen, by his second wife, Lady Susan Murray, daughter of John, first Duke of Atholl. By her Duke Cosmo had three sons, Alexander, who succeeded him; Lord William, who served in the army, was Vice Admiral of Scotland, &c., &c.; and Lord George, notorious for his connection with the "no Popery" riots in London, in 1780.

After the death of this duke in 1752, his widow married Major, afterwards General, Staats L. Morris, M.P., without issue, and died in 1779.

It is said that when the question arose of providing a jointure-house for the duchess, the duke's executors were in doubt whether to repair the old castle, or to build a new house near it. They probably saved in expense by erecting Huntly Lodge, which they decided on doing, but it is much to be regretted that so noble a specimen of an ancient Scottish mansion of the first class, as that of Huntly, should have been given over not only to decay but to spoliation. It is believed to have furnished much of the material of which Huntly Lodge was built, and it seems to have been the quarry of the district for half-a-century afterwards.

Alexander, fourth duke, succeeded his father when nine years of age. He lived in stirring and anxious times, in which Britain was almost continually at war, and few men used the influence their position conferred on them, to better purpose for the good of their country. The duke raised two line-regiments—the old 89th, afterwards reduced, and the renowned 92nd (at first numbered the 100th), or Gordon Highlanders; also, in 1778-93, two Highland Fencible Regiments—all recruited on the lands of which he was lord superior, or those immediately adjoining them. He was a knight of the Thistle, keeper of the Great Seal of Scotland, and lord-lieutenant of Aberdeenshire. He married, in 1767, Jane, daughter of Sir William Maxwell of Monreith, Bart.—celebrated for her beauty; by whom he had five daughters—Lady Charlotte married to the fourth Duke of Richmond; Lady Madelina, to Sir Robert Sinclair of Stevenston, secondly to Charles Palmer, Esq.; Lady Susan, to the Duke of Manchester; Lady Louisa, to the second Marquis of Cornwallis; Lady Georgina, to John, Duke of Bedford; and one surviving son, George, Marquis of Huntly, fifth and last Duke of Gordon, who succeeded to his father on his death in 1827.

For four hundred and fifty years the "gay Gordons" had had "the guidin' o't" over a large part of northern Scotland. It was fitting that the last representative of the leaders of this great race should possess the qualities suited to his position, and worthy of the line from which he sprung; and no one of his predecessors, probably, was more gifted with popular qualities than the last duke of the Seton-Gordon line. Born in 1770, he was a soldier from his youth. In 1791 he was already a captain in the famous 42nd Highlanders; the next year was captain-lieutenant in the 3rd regiment of Footguards; and in 1794 was made lieutenant-colonel of the Gordon Highlanders, when that regiment was raised by his father. He was with it throughout the Irish rebellion, when it was said of his command—"To the immortal honour of this regiment its behaviour was such as, if it were universal among soldiers, it would render a military government amiable." He was with his regiment again in the expedition to the Helder in 1799, where he was severely wounded; and in that of Walcheren in 1809, when, being then lieutenant-general, he commanded a division. His Grace attained the rank of full general in the army, received the Grand Cross of the Bath, was colonel of the 42nd Highlanders and afterwards of the Scots Fusilier Guards, governor of Edinburgh Castle, lord-lieutenant of Aberdeenshire, &c., &c. He married, in 1813, Elizabeth, only child and heiress of Alexander Brodie of Arnhall, by his wife, Lady Eleanor Wemyss Charteris; and died, without issue, 26th May, 1836.

Soon after their marriage the Marquis and Marchioness of Huntly, as they then were, settled at Huntly lodge, within sight of the old ancestral pile of Strathbogie. During the fourteen years that elapsed before the death of Lord Huntly's father caused them to remove, it continued to be their home, and to be the seat of a noble and far-reaching hospitality which, together with the unaffected kindliness of both host and hostess, gained for them, from all classes in the country, an esteem and respect much beyond mere popularity. It was the same when, in after years, they removed to Gordon Castle; and it must be emphatically said that, in filling the duties of his station, the duke was ever nobly seconded by the lady who was to him a most fitting partner. Her character and presence brightened his life at Gordon Castle, as it had in their earlier home; while they chastened and dignified the hospitality and the habits of life that, half-a-century ago, were too often the better of some restraint.

A gallant soldier, a true and high-bred gentleman, genial, joyous, and warm-hearted, George, Duke of Gordon, enjoyed his position, and he enjoyed keenly the discharge of its duties. Whether as representative of the crown as lord-lieutenant, as landlord, or as country gentleman, the reliance on him was unbounded. All felt they had a friend in "George of Huntly," as old people called him, one that would never be wanting in any duty; and it is little wonder that this personal affection was equalled by the universal grief that overspread the country when he, the last of the Dukes of Gordon, passed away.

After the death of the duke, his widow returned to Huntly Lodge, the scene of her early married existence. It was her home for the twenty-nine years she survived her husband; and where she lived a retired life, conspicuous only for unaffected goodness and large-hearted Christian charity—beloved and respected in no common degree. Not long after the death of her husband, the duchess resolved on raising a memorial which might perpetuate his name and her own in the place where they had passed so many happy years, and among a people between whom and themselves there existed a strong attachment. This she decided should take the form of an institution which would benefit the town of Huntly and its neighbourhood. Accordingly, her Grace built and endowed "The Gordon Schools," a handsome building at the north end of the town, consisting of a central clock-tower, pierced by an archway (through which passes the avenue to the old castle and to Huntly Lodge), with school and teachers' houses extending right and left. Busts in marble of the duke and duchess, presented by the Gordon tenantry and townspeople of Huntly, occupy niches on either side, within the archway.

On the outer and reverse sides, over the arch, are these commemorative inscriptions:—

"Gordon Schools, erected in memory of George, 5th Duke of Gordon, by his widow, Founded 1839—opened 1841,"

the other, alluding to the busts before mentioned, runs,

"These memorials of George, fifth Duke of Gordon,
and his widow, Elizabeth, Duchess of Gordon,
are placed here in testimony of the respect and affection
of an attached tenantry and a faithful people."

On the death of the fifth duke the principal title became extinct. The Huntly and Gordon Castle estates passed to the duke's nephew, Charles, fifth Duke of Richmond, K.G., who assumed, additionally, the surname and arms of Gordon. His son, the present Duke of Richmond, K.G., was created, in 1876, Duke of Gordon in the peerage of Great Britain. The Marquisate and Earldom of Huntly, with the Earldom of Enzie, along with the great Highland estates in Badenoch and Lochaber, devolved on George, fifth Earl of Aboyne, descended from Lord Charles Gordon, fourth son of the second Marquis. His grandson, Charles Gordon, is now the sixteenth Earl and eleventh Marquis of Huntly, and seventh Earl of Aboyne.

XX.

INVERCAULD.

THE Mansion House of Invercauld occupies a commanding situation, and is a conspicuous object in the view from the summit of Lochnagar, as well as from various others of the mountains of Upper Deeside. In the year 1875 were completed a series of additions and alterations, which had been in progress for some years under the superintendence of Mr. J. T. Wimperis, architect, London, and is now one of the most commodious as well as elegant residences in the north The style is the Scottish baronial, and the principal feature of the structure is the tower, which rises to a height of about seventy feet to the battlements, together with the staircase and other turrets, and a flag tower. In carrying out the extensions as much as possible of the old mansion was preserved, two or three additional storeys being added in some parts. In particular the old historic dining-hall is preserved. A broad staircase leads to an upper hall, or gallery, which is thirty-three feet long by fifteen wide. At the end of it is the drawing-room, from the windows of which an almost unrivalled panoramic view of the Deeside Highlands is obtained.

The family of Invercauld is said to derive its descent from Shaw Macduff, younger son of one of the Thanes of Fife of the middle ages. The history of the Clan Chattan, one of the branches of which is represented by the Farquharsons, is the subject of a voluminous history, into which myth and questionable tradition largely enter, and there seems to be no adequate authority for the alleged connection of Macduff with this famous clan or confederation of clans. The name Mackintosh, which was borne by the captains of this clan, signifies literally "son of the thane," and Dr. W. F. Skene* argues that the name was probably derived from the thanes of Brass or Birse, who may also have been thanes of Rothiemurchus. A precept, addressed by King Robert the Second, in 1382, to his son, Alexander Stuart, Lord of Badenoch, directs him to restrain Farchard MacToschy and

* *Celtic Scotland*, iii., 358.

his people from disturbing the Bishop of Aberdeen, and his tenants in the lands of Brass, and to oblige him to prosecute his claims by form of law. "The representatives of these older Mackintoshes," observes Dr. Skene, "were, beyond doubt, the Shaws of Rothiemurchus, and the Farquharsons of Strathdee, who extended from Badenoch as far as Birse, and whose head, in 1464, was Alexander Keir Mackintosh." One of Alexander's younger sons was Farchard or Farquhar, who settled in the Braes of Mar. Donald, *Farquhar's son*, succeeded him, and, by his marriage with a daughter of Duncan Stuart, succeeded also to a portion of the lands, afterwards known as Invercauld. The next in succession was Findla, son of the last-named, and from his great size and strength commonly called Findla-Mhor or great Findla. The courage and energy of Findla were in keeping with his magnificent physique, and in the course of his career his powers were often tried in the feuds and strifes that arose out of the jealousies of neighbours, who regarded him as an interloper. At the expense of some bloodshed he vindicated his rights, and secured himself in peaceful and prosperous possession. By his appointment as bailie of Strathdee his power was greatly extended, his vigorous administration of justice making him a terror to evildoers, while his services to the cause of law and order were rewarded by various grants of land as additions to his now extensive domains. Findla's career was brought to a close by his death in the battle of Pinkie (1547), where he is said to have carried the banner of Scotland. This, however, must have been exceptional, as the Scrymgeours of Dudhope were, from the 13th century, the hereditary standard bearers of Scotland. By his two marriages Findla had a large family, and was the common ancestor of the Farquharsons of Whitehouse, Finzean, Castleton, Monaltrie, Inverey, and Balmoral, while others of his descendants settled in the counties of Perth and Forfar. In Invercauld he was succeeded by his son, William Farquharson, who, in the reign of James VI., was succeeded by his eldest son, John, whose only son, and successor, Robert, survived till the time of Charles II. This Robert Farquharson of Invercauld, who was married to a daughter of Erskine of Pittodrie, held for some years after 1650, the barony of Wardes in Kennethmont, which he ultimately sold. By an agreement, dated the 15th October, 1651, come to at Wardhouse between him and representatives of the presbyteries of Alford and Garioch, the parishes of Insch and Kennethmont were "rectified" by the transfer of the lands of Wrays from the former to the latter, and the lands of Rochmuriel from the latter to the former. His daughter, Marjory, became the wife of George Leith of Overhall. Robert was succeeded by his son, Alexander, who married a daughter of Mackintosh

of that ilk, chief of the Clan Chattan. Their eldest son, William, dying unmarried, was succeeded by his brother, John, who was in possession when the Earl of Mar raised his standard at Castleton in 1715. Invercauld was an active, though it is believed unwilling, participant in Mar's movement; the astute Earl, who was his feudal superior, having contrived to involve him deeply in it, by constituting him one of its leaders. The chiefs of the clans met in the dining hall of Invercauld House, to concert their plans or receive their instructions; it was from Invercauld that Mar's address calling out the Highlanders was dated and issued;* and thence, for nearly the last time, the "fiery cross" was sent through the Scottish mountains. Invercauld led Mar's own regiment at Preston, and with a hundred men he boldly held a bridge against a superior force; but the fortune of the day was adverse, and along with other Jacobite chiefs he was taken prisoner and lodged in the Marshalsea Prison, where he remained till 1717. His release was hastened by the influence with the government of Mr. Ferguson, minister of Logierait, who had been incumbent of Crathie, and was the father of Dr. Adam Ferguson, the historian. In commemoration of this friendly intervention and of the clemency of the Government, Invercauld founded a benefaction, which still exists, for assisting in the maintenance and education of deserving lads of the name of Farquharson, Ferguson, or McDonald, in the parish of Crathie.† At the date of the rising of 1745, John Farquharson of Invercauld was still alive at the venerable age of seventy-six years. He disapproved of this new attempt to reinstate the Stuart dynasty, and his eldest son, James Farquharson, who was a military officer in the service of the Government also held aloof from it. Most of the Farquharson connection, however, "went out," under the leadership of the laird of Monaltrie. Invercauld's eldest daughter, Anne, the wife of her distant relative, Mackintosh of Mackintosh, exerted herself actively in the cause of the Prince, and with no little skill and courage, defeated the design of the Earl of Loudon to capture him at Moy castle some time before the battle of Culloden.

In 1750, at the age of fourscore years, John Farquharson died. He had a worthy successor in his son James, who devoted himself to the works of peace in the administration and improvement of the estate, which shortly before his accession had been augmented by the purchase of the lands of Castleton, forming part of the forfeited estates of the Earl of Mar, and by the reversion of Monaltrie on the conviction of the last laird for high treason. James Farquharson, who married the

* See "*Kildrummie.*"
† Michie: "*Deeside Tales,*" *p. 41.*

widow of the eighth Lord Sinclair and daughter of Lord George Murray, lieutenant-general of Prince Charles's army, was predeceased by all his children except one daughter, the wife of Captain James Ross, R.N., second son of Sir John Lockhart Ross of Balnagowan. On the accession of his wife to the estate, on the death of her father, in 1806, Captain Ross assumed the name of Farquharson. The estates next devolved upon their son, James Farquharson, the father of Colonel James Ross Farquharson of Invercauld, the present proprietor, while the chiefship of the clan passed to the male representative of its founder, Farquharson of Finzean, that dignity, by tribal law, not being capable of transmission through a female.

XXI.

INVERUGIE.

INVERUGIE derives its Celtic name from its position at the confluence of the river Ugie with the sea. Its earliest mention in our records is in a charter of about A.D. 1200, by which "the Church of Inverugyn, with the Chapel of Fetherangus, was given to the Monks of St. Thomas, at Arbroath, by Ralph le Neym," a member of a family which flourished in north-eastern Scotland, as well as in Tweeddale, for a century, dating from 1153. But in the reign of King William the Lion, Inverugie passed to the Cheynes*—whether by marriage or purchase is unknown—and it continued to be the head castle of that powerful family until it passed by an heiress to the Keiths, about the middle of the fourteenth century.

Where the residence and stronghold of the earlier possessors was situated is mostly conjectural. Some remains of building nearer the sea than the present ruins, were thought in the last century to have been its site. It may be so, and the Keiths may have occupied it for some generations after John Keith, brother of Sir Edward the marischal, married Mariota Cheyne. But we find, in 1491, that Sir Gilbert Keith of Inverugie and Janet Grahame, his wife, in a charter granting them the superiority of Ravenscraig, &c. (otherwise called the Craig of Inverugie, about half-a-mile west of Inverugie Castle), had licence from King James IV. to build a castle or fortalice on the Craig, "with battlements, machicoling, portcullis, and drawbridge." They and their descendants probably resided there until the marriage of the fourth Earl Marischal with Elizabeth, eldest co-heiress of her father, Sir William Keith of Inverugie, which estate, with others, she brought to her husband. We find that she

---

* Reginald le Chen was sheriff of the Mearns in 1264; and "Fermer of the Thanage of Fermartyn" in 1266. He was apparently still sheriff in 1290. The family possessed—besides Inverugie—Esslemont, Arnage, Straloch, Duffus in Morayshire, &c., &c.

In "A View of the Diocese of Aberdeen," printed by the Spalding Club, the writer (whose name appears to have been "Al. Keith") says he had been told the Earls Marischal had had the original charter of William the Lion (1165-1214) granting Inverugie. "Bernardo Cani, filio Gulielmi Canis,"—"which shews," he observes, "that *Chien* (as it was wrote of old) is the true name." This is undeniable, as the charters merely Latinized the name of the individual.

and the earl gave a charter to her paternal uncle, John Keith of Ravynniscrag, of various lands, including "the lands of Ravynscrag, with the rock and fortalice, or castle, &c., &c.,"—lying in the barony of Inverugie and sheriffdom of Aberdeen. This charter was confirmed by Queen Mary of Guise in 1543. John Keith was, of course, to hold Ravenscraig as vassal of the Earl and Countess Marischal,—but it is evident that he was to be the occupant of the castle, and it is probable that the Inverugie of the present day was then, partly at least, erected, as no portion of the building can claim a greater antiquity. It was largely added to and improved in the following century, and must have been an imposing and commodious pile, although the state of melancholy ruin in which it now is precludes any very detailed description. But a square central mass, with two corner towers, still rising to some height, give a certain impression of desolated grandeur; and the gateway and double court, with walls handsomely coped and shewing still remains of ornament, indicate some appreciation of the increased refinement in our way of living, which began to show itself in the seventeenth century.

There are no coats of arms left on the ruins. The only original sculpture is a curious representation, on a long-shaped stone, of a coach and four with two outriders preceding it, and the date 1670, which is built into one of the outer walls—one which possibly had enclosed the stable-yard. After the rising in 1715, in which the last Earl Marischal took part, the estate was forfeited, and the house fell gradually into the ruinous condition in which we see it.* It had then belonged to the Keiths for nearly three-and-a-half centuries.

The first on record † of that far-descended and popular family, is called in the charters, "Herveius filius Warini,"—a name which suggests the Norman family of Fitz Warine as his parent stock. He may have been one of the southern immigrants who were encouraged by King David I. to settle in his territories. He certainly appears as a witness to charters of that monarch (1124-53), notably to his grant of Annandale to Robert de Brus. He had a royal charter of half the lands of Keith

---

*A "prophecy"—attributed, of course, to Thomas the Rhymer, whose knowledge of Scottish localities would appear to have been ubiquitous—runs—

"Inverugie by the sea
Lordless sall your lands be,
And underneath your hearth stane
The tod sall bring her bairns hame."

† The Keiths have not escaped the fate that has befallen most of our historical families, in having a mythical origin assigned to them. The heralds of the middle ages, not discountenanced by the chroniclers, seem to have invented a set of legends, which—however grateful to their patrons, to whom history was a sealed book; and, indeed, to our forefathers generally, who received them as genuine tradition, and which, moreover, are not wanting in picturesqueness—unfortunately shrink into nothing when tested by the evidence of authentic record.

Laverockie Castle

in East Lothian, which he called Keith-Hervei, to distinguish it from the other half belonging to Symon Fraser, who had named his portion Keith-Symon.

The son of Hervei Fitz Warine (assuming that to have been his patronymic) was also called Hervei; but he appears to have followed the prevailing custom of that time, and assumed a territorial surname from the lands he held from the crown. He had the office of king's marischal, and, as Herveius de Keith, witnessed various charters of Malcolm IV. and William the Lion; but died before 1195, in which year his grandson, Philip of Keith, is called Great Marischal of Scotland. He died about 1220, having married Eda, daughter and heiress of Hugh Loreus and his wife, Eda Fraser, who had inherited Keith-Symon from her father. The whole lands of Keith-Marischal, as it then began to be called, were thus secured to the family.

Fourth in descent from this Philip was Sir Robert Keith, also Great Marischal—that office having now become hereditary in his family. He accepted a charter of the lands of Keith-Marischal, in 1294, from John Baliol; but seems to have joined the patriotic party before 1300, as he was a prisoner in England in that year. He was one of the commissioners chosen by the Scottish nation, for the settlement of their government in 1305; and a "Justiciary from the Forth to the Month." He was one of the guardians of Scotland the same year; joined the standard of King Robert Bruce; and, for his services at the battle of Inverurie and, generally, to the royal cause, he received a grant of various lands, including—besides his ancestral estate of Keith-Marischal—the forest of Kintore, with the royal hunting-seat called Hall-of-the-Forest, and other lands in Aberdeenshire and elsewhere; together with the confirmation of his hereditary office of Great Marischal of Scotland. Sir Robert commanded the Scottish cavalry at Bannockburn; and, by the king's command, made the flank attack on the English archers which so largely contributed to the victory. He was one of the "Magnates Scotiæ" who signed, in 1320, the famous letter to the pope, asserting the independence of Scotland; and ended a brilliant and patriotic career at the battle of Dupplin, where he fell, in 1332.

Sir Robert's descendants failing in the person of his grandson, Robert Keith, Great Marischal, who was killed at the battle of Durham, 1346—the succession devolved upon Sir Edward Keith, brother of Sir Robert—who left two sons—Sir William who succeeded him; and John who, by marriage with Marlota, heiress of Sir Reginald Cheyne of Inverugie and widow of John Douglas of Strathbrock, got with her both these baronies, and was ancestor of the Keiths of Inverugie and Ludquharn, of whom afterwards.

Space will not admit of record of the numerous daughters of the house of Keith; but their marriages allied it with the most distinguished families in Scotland.

Sir William Keith, eldest so nof Sir Edward, married Margaret, grand-daughter and eventually heiress of Sir Alexander Fraser, high-chamberlain of Scotland, whose wife was the Princess Mary, sister of King Robert Bruce. He acquired through his wife great estates—the forest of Collie or Cowie, the thanedom of Durris, with the baronies of Stratheychin (Strachan), and others in the Mearns. He and his wife, Margaret Fraser, made an excambion with William Lyndesay, lord of Byres, by which they obtained part of the barony of Dunnottar, adjoining their territory of Collie, &c., in exchange for Uchterutherstruther, Markinch, and Pettendrieth—in Fife and Stirlingshires. They built the castle of Dunnottar—on the site of an old Celtic fort—which became the chief residence and stronghold of the family. They had several sons, of whom the eldest, John, married a daughter of King Robert II., but left, ultimately no descendants. Their second son, another Sir Robert—(they were a truly "knightly" family)—therefore carried on the line. The third son, Alexander, had charters of various lands near Aberdeen—Grandoun (now Grandholm), Prossly (Persley), Auchmolyn (Auchmull), Crabistoun, and Balmady—from King Robert III. He commanded the cavalry of the Earl of Mar's army at the battle of Harlaw.

Sir Robert Keith, who eventually succeeded, had charters from King Robert II., in 1375, of the forest of Colly, the forest of the Month, the barony of Stratheychin (Strachan), with the forests of the same, and other lands in the Mearns. He had also a charter from Robert, Duke of Albany (who had married his sister), of the barony of Troup; and one from his father, Sir William, of the barony of Keith in East Lothian, also of the forest of Kintore, and others in Aberdeenshire, confirmed in 1406. He had married the heiress of Troup; and his second son, John, received that barony as his patrimony.

Sir Robert Keith's eldest son, Sir William, had crown charters of all his great estates in 1442-4. He was created by King James II., Earl Marischal, in or before 1458, and died before 1476. By his wife, Mary, daughter of Sir Robert Hamilton of Cadzow, he had several sons, and was succeeded by the second surviving, William, second Earl Marischal, who by his wife, Muriella, daughter of Thomas Lord Erskine, had William, third earl; Alexander of Auquhorsk, ancestor of that family; and John of Craig, who also left descendants. William, third Earl Marischal, married in 1482, Lady Elizabeth Gordon, daughter of the second Earl of Huntly. His eldest son, Robert Lord Keith, fell at Flodden, 1513; the second, William, had a charter of Troup, 1493. He also fell at Flodden. The third, Gilbert, succeeded to his brother in

Troup. The fourth, Alexander, was ancestor of the Keiths of Ravelstoun. Robert, Lord Keith's eldest son, William, succeeded his grandfather as fourth Earl Marischal. He was, apparently, one of the leading nobles of Scotland—accompanied King James V. to France, 1536, was made an Extraordinary Lord of Session, 1541, fought at Pinkie, 1547, supported the Reformation in the Scottish Parliament, 1560, was appointed a Lord of Session for the second time, 1561, and continued in offic till 1573.

"During the unhappy transactions that followed the differences between Queen Mary and Lord Darnley the Earl Marischal, wisely thinking that the post of honour was a private station, retired to his castle of Dunottar, from whence he seldom stirred, and from which he was called 'William of the Tower.' His landed property, then extending to 270,000 merks of yearly rent, lay in so many counties it was said he could travel from Berwick to the northern extremity of Scotland, eating every meal and sleeping every night upon his own estates."

The earl died in 1581, having married Margaret, daughter, and co-heir with her sister, Elizabeth, wife of Lord Forbes, of Sir William Keith of Inverugie, with whom he got that estate, on which, doubtless, there stood a castle at that date, although whether any part of it is included in the ruin still left is doubtful. His eldest son, William, Lord Keith, died the year before his father. He had married Lady Elizabeth Hay, the daughter of a near neighbour to Inverugie, George, sixth Earl of Errol, by which he had four sons and as many daughters. The earl's second son, Robert, was Commendator of the Abbey of Deer. He had the Abbey lands and baronies granted to him, and was created Lord Altrie in 1587, but left no male issue, and the title and lands devolved, in terms of his patent and charter, on his nephew, George, fifth Earl Marischal, who had succeeded his grandfather, at his death in 1581, and who, from his munificent endowment of the seat of learning in New Aberdeen, named after him, did more to perpetuate the memory of his race than all its other members through the many ages it has endured.

George, fifth Earl Marischal, was educated at some of the foreign universities, travelled and visited foreign courts—but being, according to contemporary panegyrists, greatly addicted to study, he spent much of his time at Paris and at Geneva in improving the culture which had been well begun at King's College, Old Aberdeen. At Geneva he profited by the tuition of Beza, the distinguished reformer, from whom he derived much instruction in divinity, history, and elocution. His manners and appearance are described as grave and dignified, befitting a refined and cultivated personage. But after his accession to the title, at the age of twenty-seven, the earl appears, notwithstanding his leaning towards higher pursuits, not to have been able to avoid what seems to have been in his age the inevitable consequence of high feudal position—embroilments with his neighbours, and that not without bloodshedding. Thus, in 1585, we find the Earl Marischal obtaining, along with twenty others, a remission under the great seal, for being "art and part" in the slaughter of his kinsman, William Keith, apparent of Ludquharn; and, in 1595, he is charged before the King and Privy Council as being at blood-feud with the laird of Meldrum. He behaved somewhat unsatisfactorily with respect to the actors in the Gowrie conspiracy, first supporting and then turning against them, but King James VI. saw fit to condone this inconsistency, and sent him as ambassador to Copenhagen to negotiate his marriage with the Princess Anne of Denmark. In the Memoirs of Sir James Melville are given many details respecting the king's strange vacillation and the Earl Marischal's difficulties, but all ended happily at last, and the earl acquired much credit by his able diplomacy.

In 1583 the Earl Marischal had been appointed one of the commissioners for the "new erection" and alteration in management of King's College, Old Aberdeen. It is believed that the insight he then gained into the working of such institutions, combined with his love of learning, to prompt him to found another establishment of the same kind in the more populous centre of the New Town. The foundation-charter was granted by the earl in April, 1593, was approved by the General Assembly in the same month, and was ratified by Parliament the following year.

On the rising of the "Popish lords," before the battle of Glenlivet, the Earl Marischal was appointed by the king his commissioner in the north-eastern counties, to preserve the peace and to enquire into the conduct of the insurgent leaders. Again, in 1609, he was named Lord High Commissioner to the Scottish Parliament. This seems to have been among the last of his public duties. He lived, however, till 1622, when he died at Dunnottar, enjoying in no common degree the veneration of his cotemporaries. But "the lights and shadows of Scottish life," even among those highest in place and fame, were strongly marked two-and-a-half centuries ago, and we find that the closing days of even so distinguished a man did not pass without sad molestation. "His death-bed was disturbed by the desertion and crime of an unfeeling wife," and the records of our criminal trials (Pitcairn's) tell us that:—
"On the 3rd day of March, 1624, Dame Margaret Ogilvie, Countess-Dowager of Marischal, along with her then husband, Sir Alexander Strachan of Thorntoun, Knight, and Robert Strachan, doctor of physic, were accused before the High Court of Justiciary of the ignoble crimes of masterful theft and stouthrief, in having stolen

from the place of Benholm, belonging to the earl, certain jewels, silver-plate, household stuff, gold, silver, and title-deeds, in October, 1622, a little before the said earl's decease." On the same day James Keith of Benholm, eldest son of the earl by this, his second wife, was cited to answer for a similar crime, committed at the same time and in the same place. The two cases are evidently connected together, and the minute in the latter gives an inventory of the articles stolen which is a remarkable evidence of the magnificence and wealth of the earl, surely very exceptional in so poor a country as Scotland then was, although it was beginning in some degree to prosper, since peace with England had become the rule. Some of the items are, "Portugal ducats and other species of foreign gold, to the avail of 2,600 pounds, or thereby; thirty-six dozen gold buttons; the Queen of Denmark's picture set in gold, set about with rich diamonds, estimated at 5000 merks; a chain of 'equall perle,' wherein were four hundred pearls, great and small; two chains of gold of twenty-four ounce weight; another jewel of diamonds set in gold, worth 3000 merks; a great pair of bracelets all set with diamonds, price thereof 600 crowns, &c., &c., &c.; also 16,000 merks of silver and gold ready coined, &c." The plunderers also helped themselves to "the whole tapestry, silver-work, bedding, goods, gear, and plenishing within the said place" of Dunnottar; and yet it is on record that, excepting that Keith of Benholm was outlawed for non-appearance when summoned, they seem to have wholly evaded restitution or punishment—a failure of justice savouring strongly of corruption in the Scottish law-officers of the period.

George, fifth Earl Marischal, died the 5th April, 1623—(his widow had already taken her second husband, who had assisted in robbing her first, before March, 1624)—and a funeral oration was read at Marischal College on the 30th June following, by the Professor (Ogstoun) who held the Chair of Moral Philosophy. A "Book of Tears," bearing a lengthy and complimentary title, was written and published in the same year, composed by Massy, Alexander Wedderburn, and others, and printed by Raban at Aberdeen.

William, sixth Earl Marischal, eldest son of Earl George, gave a charter of Novodamus to Marischal College. He had, as was usual, charters of his baronies of Inverugie, Dunottar, Altrie, &c., &c., in 1612; of the barony of Keith-Marischal in Nova Scotia, 1625; of the lands of Kynellar, 1627; and of Benholm the same year. He was of the Privy Council of Charles I.; and—a curious act for a subject—he is said to have, in 1634, "fitted out a fleet, which he sent to Uladislans, King of Poland." He died in 1635. By his wife, Lady Margaret Erskine of Mar, he left, with other children, William, seventh Earl Marischal, who espoused the cause of the Covenant, but eventually sided with Charles II. He was forfeited by Cromwell, but was reinstated in his possessions at the Restoration, soon after which he died, leaving daughters only. His next brother, George, succeeded him as eighth earl; another brother, John, was created Earl of Kintore.

The eighth Earl Marischal served in his youth in the French army, but returned to this country in time to take part in the Civil War, in which, like his brother and predecessor, he fought for the Crown, commanding a regiment at Preston, and a brigade at the battle of Worcester. He lived till 1694, and left, by his wife, Lady Mary Hay of Kinnoul, an only child, William, ninth earl, who, marrying Lady Mary Drummond, eldest daughter of James, fourth Earl of Perth, left two sons, George, nth earl, and James, afterwards the celebrated general; also two daughters, Lady Mary Keith, married, in 1711, to John, sixth Earl of Wigton,* and Lady Anne, said to have been "justly esteemed for her wit and beauty, and all the qualities worthy of her noble birth," who married Alexander, sixth Earl of Galloway.

George, tenth and last Earl Marischal, was born about 1693, and succeeded his father, in 1712, in his titles and office of Great Marischal of Scotland, but in the estates of Dunnottar, Fetteresso, and Inverugie only, the rest of the great possessions of the Keiths having been dilapidated during Cromwell's usurpation, or given off in provisions to younger branches of the family. He commanded the troop of Scottish lifeguards under Queen Anne, and is said to have offered to proclaim "King James" at its head. Finding there was no movement in favour of the Stuart prince, however, he made up his mind to recognise George I.; but was, not unjustifiably, deprived of his command. At the same time his kinsman, the Earl of Mar, was dismissed from his office of Secretary of State. This treatment, along with the advice of his mother, who was a Roman Catholic and a Jacobite, had the unfortunate effect of drawing the earl and his brother over to the party adhering to the Stuarts. They received the "Chevalier de St. George" at Fetteresso, and attended him in his progress southwards; and having served under Lord Mar at Sheriffmuir, and throughout the rising of 1715, attainder and forfeiture were the consequence. They escaped abroad, taking refuge in France and Spain successively. They joined in the attempt to raise the Highlands for "King James" in 1719, and fought at Glenshiel. Again escaping to the Continent they eventually reached Spain once more, where they seem to have been allowed pay as military officers, though without definite employment. They paid at least one visit to the "Chevalier de St. George" at Rome, but

---

* They had one daughter, Lady Clementina Fleming, married to Charles, tenth Lord Elphinstone, and had issue. One of her sons, Sir George Keith Elphinstone, K.B., the well-known naval commander, was created Baron Keith of Stonehaven Marischal.

without improvement to their prospects—their master, as they held him to be, having little power or means to help his exiled friends. After many vicissitudes, the Earl Marischal obtained employment in the service of Frederick the Great of Prussia, of whom he became the much trusted friend, and who certainly shewed an amount of attachment towards the earl that he rarely, if ever, accorded to anyone. Frederick gave him the government of Neufchatel, in Switzerland, that canton being then an appanage of the House of Hohenzollern, and where the Keith arms may still be seen, among others, in the town-hall of that picturesque city. The earl also filled at different times the position of ambassador from Prussia to Paris, and to Madrid. While resident at the latter place, in 1759, he was so fortunate as to discover the existence of the "Family Compact," a secret alliance of the different branches of the Bourbon family. As this was likely to injure the interests of Great Britain, Lord Marischal determined on giving the important information to the elder Pitt, who was then prime-minister, as his doing so in no way effected the interests of Prussia. This service was considered so valuable, that King George II. accorded him a free pardon for his former treasonable acts, and a reversal of his attainder speedily followed. The earl also received a grant of public money, which enabled him, in 1764, to purchase back part of his estates, Inverugie included, from the York Buildings Company. He had succeeded, in 1761, under an entail, to the estate of Keith-Hall, on the death of his cousin, the fourth Earl of Kintore; those lands having been settled on that branch of the family when the peerage was given, in 1661, but to revert to the head of the house on failure of heirs to the title of Kintore. It is said that after regaining Inverugie, he was so cast down at finding it in ruins, and the associations of his youth impossible of renewal, that he easily yielded to the earnest persuasion of Frederick, and returned to Berlin soon afterwards. He there spent an honoured old age, and died in 1778, aged eighty-five, enjoying to the last the regard of his contemporaries, and notably that of the king, of whom it was said that he never loved but one man, and that was the Scottish Earl Marischal.

The earl had survived his brother twenty years; and, neither having been married, the title at his death became dormant, not extinct, as descendants in the male line from the earlier holders of the title, are believed to exist. He was succeeded in Kintore and Keith-Hall estates by Anthony Adrian, eighth Lord Falconer of Halkertoun, descended from Lady Catherine Keith, daughter of William, second Earl of Kintore, and wife of David, fifth Lord Halkertoun.

Thus calmly closed the life of the last of the lordly Keiths; but the family record would be imperfect without some notice of his still more distinguished brother, whose career was even more romantic and eventful than his own.

The Honourable James Keith was born in 1696. He shared with his elder brother the advantage of having been in part educated by their kinsman (afterwards) Bishop Keith. It was at first intended he should follow the law as a profession; but his preference for a military life prevailed, and in 1715 he set out for London to ask for a commission in the army. At York he met the Earl Marischal, travelling towards Scotland, in high displeasure at having had his troop of lifeguards taken from him; and it ended, as has been before said, in the two brothers joining Mar's army, and acting a distinguished part in the rebellion. For several years their history was almost identical, but their paths diverged when the elder brother obtained employment in Prussia. James Keith continued his attempts to obtain a command in the Spanish service; but—although treated generously as to unattached pay, and allowed to serve as a volunteer in the abortive siege of Gibraltar, by Spain, in 1727—his religion, for he and his brother were Protestants, proved an insurmountable bar to regular employment.

At last, after several years of hope deferred, in 1728—through the good offices of the Spanish Duke de Liria, whose friendship never failed him, and who was then ambassador from Spain to St. Petersburg—Keith was received into the service of the Czar, Peter the Second of Russia, with the rank of major-general. His new master, however, died in 1730; but the Empress Anne (Duchess of Courland and niece of Peter the Great), who succeeded him, confirmed General Keith in his rank, and gave him the command of a regiment of guards, one of the highest appointments she had to bestow. These details, and Keith's services for some years later, are drawn from a diary kept by him—unfortunately only a fragment—printed by the Spalding Club in 1843. In 1732 he was appointed one of the "Inspectors" of the army, having thirty-two regiments in his district, extending, along the Volga and Don, to the frontier of Poland, involving in his tour of duty four thousand five hundred miles of travelling. In the summer of 1733 he was in command of six thousand troops in the Ukraine, as troubles were threatening in Poland; and in December he entered that country, passing the Nieper on the ice, to assist in putting down a rising of part of the Polish nation against the newly elected king, Stanislaus, which was supposed to be contrary to Russian interests. The general distinguished himself in this expedition, not more by his skill and bravery, than by the humanity he showed towards the inhabitants of the country he was invading.

Space will not admit of more details of Keith's important services to Russia;

but they were such as show him to have been one of the most remarkable among the numbers of able and valiant Scotsmen who, in the wars of the seventeenth and eighteenth centuries, gained for their country a European reputation far beyond its importance in population or resources. Partly from the renown he had gained, and partly, no doubt, from the position the earl, his brother, held in the estimation of Frederick of Prussia, a pressing invitation from that monarch to transfer his talents to the service of Brandenburg had its effect; and he accepted a high command in Frederick's army, with the Governorship of Berlin attached to it. From thenceforth he enjoyed, like his brother, if in a less degree, the confidence and friendship of the king, who looked on him as one of his most trusty counsellors. Advanced to the rank of Field-marshal, Keith continued to add to his military reputation during the many years of his life still to run; while he preserved his genial, high-minded character in all its purity.

Such a life was not one to be thrown away; and yet it was sacrificed to a rash act of the Prussian king, the consequences of which must have caused him life-long regret. In the course of the Seven Years' War, in October, 1758, Frederick, wishing to cover Dresden from the advance of the Austrians, under Marshal Daun, who were threatening it, took up, on the 10th October, a position at Hochkirch, about twenty miles to the eastward of that city, on a range of heights facing another, which, at only a mile's distance, was occupied by the enemy, who outnumbered the Prussians by two to one. But, having defeated them at Leuthen the year before, when the odds against him were even greater—somewhat despising, too, the lack of enterprise in the Austrian commanders—the king thought he might venture on an act which would have disgraced a third-rate general. For it was evident that the superior numbers opposed to him would enable them to overlap and fall on his flanks, rendering a retreat inevitable. Keith had been absent at the moment; but on rejoining the army and finding its position so faulty, his remark was, "If Daun does not attack us here he ought to be hanged." Accordingly before daylight on the 14th, a thick fog helping to cover their movements, the enemy having massed an immense force on the Prussian right, where Keith was in command, made a furious attack on his part of the position, of which Hochkirch was the key. That village was the scene of desperate fighting, and was taken and retaken many times; but, no reinforcements arriving, the weight of numbers prevailed, and the Prussians were driven back in dire confusion, almost surrounded. This was, no doubt, aggravated by the death of their heroic leader, for Keith had led them in person in their repeated attacks and charges, encouraging them by voice and example through all. But for him the end had come;

and he fell where the fight was thickest,—a death worthy of his race. Frederick, who was far on Keith's left, does not seem to have realised the importance of the attack on Hochkirch until the mischief was done, but, even when he discovered his losses, he would not accept defeat. He drew off and rallied his broken right-wing, and fell back with his army to so good a position, nearer Dresden, that Daun thought it well to be content with the success he had gained, and try for no more. But the faithful friend of so many years, the wise counsellor, the noble-minded exile that had paid the king the highest compliment man could give, of accepting him as his master and making his country his own, was no longer at his side,—James Keith's last fight was fought, his "spur was cold."

Severely wounded during the action, he had absolutely refused to leave the field; and, while heading what appears to have been a desperate attempt to break through the Austrians with the bayonet, being surrounded and almost overwhelmed, he fell dead in the arms of his faithful English groom, shot through the heart. So inextricable was the confusion and so disastrous, that the body of the marshal could not be brought off. Sad to say it was plundered and stripped, and lay among piles of slain, until recognised by some of the Austrians who had known him in former days. Then it was reverently brought into the church of Hochkirch, where Daun and Lacy and other Austrian officers, to their honour be it said, looked with genuine sorrow on the remains of the noble foe they had admired and esteemed when in life. Lacy, who had been his personal friend, shed tears at the sight.

Carlyle's words may be fitly quoted here. "On the morrow, Sunday, October 15th, Keith had honourable soldier's burial there; 'twelve cannon' salvoing thrice, and 'the whole corps of Colloredo' with their muskets thrice; Lacy as chief-mourner, not without tears. Four months after, by royal order, Keith's body was conveyed to Berlin; reinterred in Berlin, in a still more solemn public manner, with all the honours, all the regrets; and Keith sleeps now in the Garrison-Kirche; far from bonny Inverugie: the hoarse sea-winds and caverns of Dunottar singing vague requiem to his honourable line and him, in the imagination of some few. 'My Brother leaves me a noble legacy,' said the old Lord Marischal; 'last year he had Bohemia under ransom; and his personal estate is 70 ducats' (about £25)." "In Hochkirch church there is still, not in the churchyard as formerly, a fine, modestly impressive monument to Keith; modest urn of black marble on a pedestal of grey, and, in gold letters, an inscription not easily surpassable in the lapidary way: . . . 'Dum in Prælio non procul hinc Inclinatam Suorum aciem Mente manu voce et exemplo Restituebat Pugnans ut Heroas decet occubuit. D. xiv Octobris.' These

words go through you like the clang of steel.* Friedrick's sorrow over him, ... is indeed a monument. Twenty years after Keith had from his Master a Statue, in Berlin. One of Four: to the Four most deserving; Schweriu (1771) Winterfield (1777) Seidlitz (1778) Keith (when?)—which still stand in the Wilhelm Platz there."
. . . . "Old Lord Marischal—George, 'Maréchal d' Ecosse,' as he always signs himself—was by this time seventy-two; King's Governor of Neufchâtel, for a good while past and to come (1754-63). In 'James,' the junior, but much the stronger and more solid, he has lost, as it were, a *father* and younger brother at once; . . . and the tears of the old man are natural and affecting. Ten years older than his brother and survived him still twenty years."

But we have wandered with its exiled lords far from "bonny Inverugie." We must return to it once more to say, that the castle, with the barony of St. Fergus and the old Abbey lands of Deer, were purchased from the Earl Marischal by Lord Pitfour, a Scottish judge, whose great grandson, Colonel George Arthur Ferguson, late of the Grenadier Guards, now possesses them. The modern mansion-house of these great estates, at Pitfour, forms, with its fine pleasure-grounds, gardens, and extensive woodlands, a residence not surpassed, if equalled, by any other in the County of Aberdeen.

---

* This monument was raised to Marischals' Keiths' memory by his kinsman, Colonel Sir Robert Murray Keith, K.B., who, some years after the battle of Hochkirch, was British Minister at Dresden. The inscription was written by the Italian poet, Metastasio, and the part given by Carlyle has certainly much of the old Roman fire. In their entirety the lines run :—

Jacobo Keith, Gulielmi Comitis Marescelli Hered :
Regni Scotiæ, et Mariæ Drummond, Filio,
Frederici Borussorum Regis Summo Exercitus
Præfecto; Viro Antiquis Moribus et Militari
Virtute Claro, Qui, Dum in prælio non procul
hinc, Inclinatam suorum aciem Mente, Manu,
Voce, et Exemplo Restituebat, pugnans ut Heroas
decet, Occubuit. Anno 1758—Mense Oct.

XXII.

KILDRUMMIE.

KILDRUMMIE Castle, situated in the gorge of the extensive valley through which the river Don winds its course to the eastward, and which, expanding to the north, reaches almost uninterruptedly to the base of the Hill of Noth, in Strathbogie, is celebrated in Scottish history, not only as the palace of kings, but as having been the scene of frequent and sanguinary warfare connected with its internal defence, and as the arena around which frequent battles and skirmishes were fought, the record of which is perpetuated by the tumuli that, notwithstanding modern improvement and the extension of cultivation, still mark the resting-place of the brave.

The castle has evidently not only been of great extent, but of much architectural magnificence. Unfortunately some of the finest parts of the building now exist but in their ruined basements, and the "Snow Tower," at the north-west corner of the quadrangle—by all accounts the most ancient, most important, and noblest portion of the castle—is more than any other dilapidated and fallen. Some idea of its former state may, however, be formed from the masonry of its base, the thickness of its walls, and its extensive area; nor can there exist a doubt that this must have been a conspicuous and highly ornamental feature of the building.

The entrance to the castle forms the centre of the southern face of the quadrangle; it has been flanked by towers. The court-yard is very extensive, and five towers, exclusive of those at the entrance, formerly defended the outer wall. Four of these marked the angles of this noble building. The "Snow tower" stood out more prominently from the general line of the castle than any of the others; and the fifth tower was constructed near to it, but more in a line with the western face of the fortress. The tower now in the best state of preservation is that to the north-east; and when its extent, height, and proportions are considered, some estimate may be formed of what the "Snow tower" must have been, when it greatly

surpassed in importance this certainly very fine specimen of the architecture of the time.

Kildrummie stands between two ravines, called the north and south glens. A brook issuing from the former washes the base of the eminence on which the building is placed, the ground falling precipitously towards the north, gave additional strength and protection to that part of the fabric, while a moat, encircling its western, southern, and eastern faces, by being flooded, rendered the approach of assailants more hazardous and difficult. A popular, but not well authenticated, impression has prevailed, that a subterraneous passage existed, giving egress from the vaults of the castle. This appears to be a mistake; a footpath excavated in the bank, and built up on each side, and arched, formerly led from the back of the great hall to the burn in the north glen, but the stones fallen from the building having been removed, and the pathway clearly traced out, no appearance of an entrance to the underground parts of the castle, if any such existed, could be discovered. The great hall in the northern part of the building can still be traced with accuracy, forming an oblong of seventy-three feet by forty. The chapel, with its great window to the east, is also distinctly marked, its length being thirty-five feet by twenty. The hall has contained four windows facing to the north, and at its north-east angle are the remains of a spiral staircase. The eastern front, including the towers, extends to the length of one hundred and eighty feet; the northern to two hundred and sixty-two. The distance from the chapel window to the nearest wall of the "Snow tower" is two hundred feet. The "Snow tower" is fifty-five feet in diameter, that to the north-east being in diameter thirty-four at its base. There appears to be no satisfactory record of the first construction of the castle; the original building was undoubtedly of great antiquity, nor can the additions and alterations made from time to time be authenticated until the reign of Alexander the Second, who, having appointed Saint Gilbert, bishop of Caithness, to be his treasurer in the north of Scotland, that prelate, during his tenure of office, made great additions to Kildrummie, comprising the seven towers, of which the ruins are now extant.

David, the brother of William the Lion, having been created Earl of Huntingdon in England, and of Garioch in the Scottish Peerage, the latter title carried with it in property the castle of Kildrummie.

David's second daughter, Isabella, brought it in dower to her husband, Robert Bruce, lord of Annandale; and his grandson, Robert the First, gave it to his sister, Christian, the wife of Gratney, Earl of Mar, from whom descended the royal house of Stuart.

Edward the First of England, during his progress in the north, visited the castle in 1303, and the following year Sir William Wallace, a name ever memorable in Scottish history, passed several days within its walls. In 1305 the Earl of Carrick was ordered by Edward to put the castle under a keeper, for whom he should be responsible, and in the following year Kildrummie was besieged by the English king. On that occasion Robert Bruce, himself a wanderer, after losing the battle of Methven, sent his brother Nigel and the Earl of Athol to conduct the Queen to Kildrummie, from whence, on the alarm of an immediate siege, she fled, and, accompanied by the Lady Margery, daughter of the king by a former marriage, took refuge in the monastery of St. Duthac in Ross-shire. The castle, after being gallantly defended, was surrendered in consequence of a conflagration, which, occasioned either by accident or treachery, caused the immediate fall of the place, and left the young and gallant Nigel Bruce in the hands of his enemies; he was soon after put to death at Berwick. Christopher and Alexander Seton were executed at Newcastle, and the Earl of Athol suffered the same fate in London.

Kildrummie having been recovered by Bruce, subsequently became the prison of Duncan, Earl of Fife, and his family, he having been captured at Perth, where Edward Baliol had left him in command, after gaining the battle of Dupplin.

In 1335, David Comyn, Earl of Athol, attacked the castle, but alarmed at the array of nobles leagued against him, he raised the siege, and, marching to encounter them, lost his life in the battle of Culblean. The castle of Kildrummie was, during these events, in charge of Lady Christian Bruce, who married Gratney, Earl of Mar.

In 1341, David the Second, after having been expatriated for nine years, returned from France, and on the 20th June of that year was at Kildrummie; he also visited it in August and November, 1342. He passed the autumn of 1361 and the commencement of the following year in Aberdeenshire; during the former, in consequence of a quarrel with Thomas, Earl of Mar, he besieged and took the castle. That earl having accepted a pension from the third Edward, and become a resident in England, incurred the forfeiture of his estates; upon his obtaining pardon, however, they appear to have been restored, and returning to his native land, he died at Kildrummie, and was buried under the eastern buildings of the castle. In 1365, David the Second was again at Kildrummie, but no event of importance appears to have occurred during the royal visit on that occasion.

In 1403, the castle continued to be the property of the Mar family. The Countess became in that year a widow; her husband, Sir Malcolm Drummond, brother to the late queen of Scotland, having been, when residing at Kildrummie, attacked by a band of ruffians, imprisoned in its dungeons, and subjected to treatment that speedily terminated his existence. Alexander Stuart, natural son of the Earl of Buchan, was suspected of having been the instigator to this lawless and barbarous proceeding. He soon afterwards appeared before the castle with a force of freebooters, carried it by assault, and whether by violence or persuasion obtained in marriage the widowed countess. To allay the ferment of popular opinion, and to give a favourable colour to his usurpation, this ferocious descendant of the "Wolf of Badenoch" caused the following scene to be enacted:—Stuart appeared at the gate, and was there met by the Countess of Mar, who, in presence of the Bishop of Ross, and of the vassals and tenantry, assembled for the occasion, received from him the keys of the castle, declaring that he gave them freely to be disposed of as she pleased. The countess then, as had been previously arranged, declared that she chose Alexander Stuart as her husband, and gave him in marriage the earldom of Mar, with the castle of Kildrummie, and the lands appertaining to that noble family. This act was ratified and confirmed by Robert the Third, notwithstanding the person murdered to make way for this usurpation was the brother-in-law of the king, and that no doubt existed in the public mind of Stuart having been the murderer, as he became the successful wooer of the unfortunate countess. Upon the death of Stuart, the Erskines claimed the earldom in default of heirs male; but James the Second bestowed it on his son, John, who, dying unmarried, it was given by the weak and unfortunate James the Third to his favourite, Robert Cochrane, of whose appearance and retinue Tytler gives the following description:—"His tent or pavilion was of silk, the fastening chains were richly gilt; he was accompanied by a body guard of three hundred stout retainers in sumptuous liveries, and armed with light battle-axes; a helmet of exquisitely polished steel, and richly inlaid with gold, was borne before him, and when not armed for the field, he wore a riding suit of black velvet, with a massive gold chain round his neck, and a hunting horn, tipped with gold and adorned with precious stones, across his shoulder." Upon the death of this minion, whom the confederate nobles, led by Douglas, Earl of Angus, hanged over the parapet of the Bridge of Lauder, James the Third bestowed the earldom of Mar upon his son John, notwithstanding the claims of the Erskines, originally advanced in 1436, and Sir Robert Erskine, in support of that claim, having in 1442 besieged and taken the castle of Kildrummie. Upon its becoming again at the disposal of the crown, it was bestowed by Mary Queen of Scots upon her natural brother, James Stuart, the celebrated Regent Murray; but during the differences which occurred in those times of barbarism, turbulence, and intrigue, Mary, in 1565, five years previous to the assassination of Murray, recognized the claim of the Erskines, and the Mar title has continued in that family to the present time.

John Erskine, the Earl of Mar of 1715, succeeded to the title in 1712; he was the following year appointed a secretary of state by Queen Anne; but after her death, deserting the service of the house of Hanover, he erected the standard of the Stuarts at Braemar, in 1715, fought the doubtful battle of Sheriffmuir, subsequently escaped to France, was attainted in 1716, and the forfeiture of his estates occasioned the castle of Kildrummie to pass into other hands. During the period of his command of the Highland army, and after having erected the standard of the Stuarts at Braemar, disappointed at his vassals not following the example of their lord, he addressed the following letter to the bailie of Kildrummie—a document very characteristic of the power exercised by a feudal baron of the time :—

Invercauld, Sept. 9 at night, 1715.

Jocke,—Ye was in the right not to come with the hundred men ye sent up to night, when I expected four times the number. It is a pretty thing, when all the Highlands of Scotland are now rising upon their king and country's account, as I have accounts from them since they were with me, and the gentlemen of our neighbouring Lowlands expecting us down to join them, that my men should be only refractory. Is not this the thing we are now about, which they have been wishing these twenty-six years? And now, when it is come, and the king and country's cause is at stake, will they for ever sit still and see all perish? I have used gentle means too long, and so shall be forced to put other orders I have in execution. I have sent you enclosed and order for the lordship of Kildrummy, which you are immediately to intimate to all my vassals; if they give ready obedience, it will make some amends, and if not, ye may tell them from me, that it will not be in my power to save them (were I willing) from being treated as enemies, by those who are ready soon to join me; and they may depend on it, that I will be the first to propose and order their being so. Particularly, let my own tenants in Kildrummy know, that if they come not forth with their best arms, that I will send a party immediately to burn what they shall miss taking from them. And they may believe this only a threat, but by all that's sacred, I'll put it in execution, let my loss be what it will, that it may be an example to others. You are to tell the gentlemen that I'll expect them in their best accoutrements, on horseback, and no excuse to be excepted of. Go about this with all diligence, and come yourself and let me know your having done so. All this is not only as ye will be answerable to me, but to your king and country.

Your assured friend and servant,
MAR.

To John Forbes of Inverernan,
    Bailie of Kildrummy.

With the forfeiture of John, Earl of Mar, in 1716, terminated the connexion of that very ancient family with the castle of Kildrummie, which had so long remained their property, and subsequently of the Erskines, who succeeded to the title and estates in default of heirs male to the Mars, Earls of Mar.

In 1731, the castle and estate of Kildrummie became the property of John Gordon, of Wardhouse, by purchase from Mr. James Erskine, of Grange, advocate, and Mr. David Erskine, of Dun, one of the senators of the College of Justice, then joint proprietors of the Mar estates. In the Wardhouse family it has since continued, the present proprietor being Carlos Pedro Gordon, Esq. of Wardhouse and Kildrummie.

CASTLE FORBES.

CASTLE Forbes, formerly Putachie, and now the principal residence of the senior baron of the Scottish Peerage, is situated on the north bank of the river Don, which passes through the grounds on its course to the ocean. The castle is removed but a short distance from the south-west shoulder of Benachie, which there becomes the boundary of the Vale of Alford. Rising immediately from the river, and surrounded by extensive woodlands, the lawn slopes gradually to its banks, and the view from the house being uninterrupted, is varied and extensive.

The building is modern, in a castellated style of architecture, built of granite from designs by Archibald Simpson, and forms a striking and picturesque object from all points of the valley beneath. The late Lord Forbes erected the castle, and greatly altered and improved the place, changing its name from Putachie to its present designation.

The Forbes family are descended from John de Forbes, of the reign of William the Lion. In the year 1304, the Castle of Urquhart was obstinately defended by Alexander Forbes, against Edward I. of England, who, incensed at the resistance, upon gaining possession, put its garrison to the sword; but the family was continued by the birth of a posthumous son, afterwards killed at the battle of Dupplin, in 1382. His son, John, was succeeded by Alexander, the first Lord Forbes, and his second son, William, became the ancestor to the Lords Pitsligo, the last of whom incurred forfeiture by joining Prince Charles Edward in 1745.

Alexander, first Lord Forbes, died in 1448, and was succeeded by his son, James, the second lord, who had three sons—William, the third lord; Duncan, ancestor of the late Sir John Stuart Forbes of Pitsligo, and other families; and Patrick, ancestor of the family of Forbes of Craigievar, now Lord Sempill, and of the Earls of Granard. William, the third lord, also left three sons, of whom the eldest, Alexander, the fourth lord, acted a conspicuous part in the dissensions that agitated Scotland after the murder of James III., joining the insurrection of the Earl of Lennox and other barons. Lord Forbes, indignant at the ascendancy of the favourites and parasites who then ruled the court of the fourth James, appeared in open revolt, marching through the country and displaying the blood-stained garment of the murdered king, he rallied around him multitudes who unhesitatingly joined the insurrection. The promptitude and firmness of the young monarch and his nobles terminated this formidable revolt, by surprising and entirely defeating the army of the Earl of Lennox at Galla Moss, about sixteen miles from Stirling. The clemency of James IV. was conspicuous on this occasion, and the Lord Forbes with others were not only pardoned, but restored to royal favour. Dying without issue, he was succeeded by Arthur, the fifth lord, who left no family, and his youngest brother, John, became the sixth Lord Forbes. He was in 1536 accused of high treason, and, with his son, brought to trial, charged with having conspired to murder the king by the shot of a culverin, in Aberdeen, and with having aided the English enemies of his Majesty. From this very serious accusation Lord Forbes was exculpated, and released after a long confinement. His son having been found guilty, was executed in the year 1537.

For many years great animosity and rivalry subsisted between the Gordons and the Forbeses, the consequence of which was frequent and barbarous attacks made by one party upon the lives and property of the other. Murder, spoliation, and deceit were the frequent consequences of the family differences during these barbarous times, when constant and predatory petty warfare rendered life and property insecure, and when the laws but feebly enforced the obedience of wild and reckless men to a line of conduct consistent with order and well-regulated society. On one of these occasions, Adam Gordon of Auchindoun was met at the Craibstane, near Aberdeen, by the Master of Forbes and his followers, when a furious encounter took place, both parties fighting with the inveteracy of feudal hatred. In the end the Gordons prevailed, many of the Forbeses were slain, and their leader, the master, remained the prisoner of the victors. This skirmish took place on the 20th November, 1571. In 1594, the Earls of Huntly and Errol came into hostile contact on the field of Glenlivat with the Earl of Argyll, and with a very inferior force defeated that young and inexperienced nobleman. Lord Forbes, Leslie of Balquhain, and Irvine of

Drum, having assembled their vassals for the purpose of joining the royal army under Argyll, learning the fatal termination of the battle, resolved to return home and revenge former quarrels. With this intent these parties assembled at Druminnor, then the chief seat of the Forbes family, where arrangements having been made for the contemplated foray, they set forward on their way.

But when riding by the side of Lord Forbes, one of the Irvines was shot by an unknown hand; the arms of the whole party were immediately examined, and, strange to say, every one of them found to be loaded! This prevented the possibility of identifying the murderer; but suspicion and distrust were created, and having disbanded their followers, the chiefs returned to their respective homes.

In 1597 a contract was subscribed by the Earl of Huntly and Lord Forbes, by which they agreed to bury all feuds and animosities between the families. Lord Forbes was uncle, by marriage, to Huntly, having married his aunt, Lady Margaret Gordon, daughter of the fourth earl.

On the 20th July, 1638, the Master of Forbes accompanied the Marquis (then Earl) of Montrose to Aberdeen, calling upon its inhabitants to sign "The Covenant," but, notwithstanding the authority with which they were invested, and the numerous harangues and exhortations that hourly assailed them, the great body of the Aberdonians refused to do so.

In the following year, the Earl of Montrose, accompanied by the Earl Marischal and General Leslie, entered Aberdeen at the head of 6000 men, where his force was augmented by the arrival of Lord Fraser, the Master of Forbes, and other Aberdeenshire barons, with a reinforcement of 2000 cavalry and infantry. This formidable army had in view the twofold object, to overawe the north, and to impose the oath on the refractory inhabitants of the town. William, the twelfth Lord Forbes, died in 1716, and was succeeded by his eldest son, who married the daughter of William Dale, Esq., by whom he had an only son, the fourteenth lord, who, dying a minor, in 1734, was succeeded by his uncle, James, younger son of the twelfth baron, and who became the fifteenth Lord Forbes, carrying forward the family honours in a direct line; his son married the sister of Lord Pitsligo, by whom he had James, who, upon the death of his father, became the seventeenth peer. Born in 1724, he married, in 1760, Catharine, only daughter of Sir Robert Innes, Bart. Their eldest son, James Ochoncar, the late lord, succeeded to the title and estates on the 29th July, 1804. He married in 1792, Elizabeth, daughter of Walter Hunter of Polmood, in the county of Peebles, by Caroline, fourth daughter of George, Earl of Cromarty. After being for many years in the Coldstream Guards, he became a general officer of the army, and died colonel of the Royal North British Fusileers. His lordship was for some time during the reign of George IV. his majesty's high commissioner to the General Assembly of the Church of Scotland. The Lords Forbes were created baronets of Nova Scotia in 1628, and the late General Lord Forbes, when commanding the British troops in Sicily, was decorated with the order of St. Januarius. He was also one of the sixteen representative peers of Scotland in the Imperial Parliament. His eldest son, James, having predeceased his father, the title and estates descended, in 1843, to Walter Forbes of Brux, the second son, and nineteenth baron, who was succeeded, in 1868, by his son, the present peer.

It appears from the best authenticated records, that the numerous and respectable families of the name, both in Scotland and in Ireland, are descended from the John de Forbes of the reign of William the Lion; and it is a singular fact, that so ancient a name and peerage should have regularly descended, without in one instance a collateral having inherited the honours, for a period of four hundred and fifty years.

The Forbes family are in possession of very ancient charters, and they flourished greatly in wealth and prosperity from 1371 to 1513, but afterwards declined in importance. This may in a great measure be attributed to their constant feudal strife with the Gordons, then become most powerful in the north of Scotland; but this did not tend to diminish the number of families of the name who possessed property in the country, or now to reduce in importance the noble family representing, with the exception of the Hamilton, Crauford, Huntly, Sutherland, and Mar titles, the most ancient peerage of the Scottish nobility.

XXIII.

KINNAIRD.

KINNAIRD Castle was built by Sir Alexander Fraser of Philorth, and was begun in 1570. Of the building only the tower remains, a structure thirty-nine feet long by twenty-seven wide, but rising to a height of four storeys, and furnished with battlements. Since 1787 it has been in the possession of the Commissioners of Northern Lights, by whom it has been converted into a lighthouse, for which purpose its commanding position on Kinnaird Head strongly recommended it. The light is 120 feet above high water mark, and is visible a distance of 15 miles. About 50 yards from the castle, and built over a cave called the Selch's Hole, is the Wine Tower, 25 feet long by 21 wide, and 25 feet high on the landward side, but it is of greater height towards the sea. The tower consists of two vaulted apartments, the one above the other. One of the two doors of the building is reached by an exterior wooden stair, an unusual arrangement, but not without examples in Scottish architecture. The upper room or storey has an arched window in each wall, freestone carved pendants of coats of arms ornamenting each arch. Three pendants, also of freestone, but of a more elaborate and pretentious character, are placed in the centre of the roof. One represents an eagle holding a key in his beak, the wings meeting behind, and in his talons a shield bearing the arms of Fraser and Abernethy quartered, the bird being encircled by a scroll with the words, "The glory of the honorable is to feir God." Another represents two unicorns with horns crossed in front, so as to form, with two swords, a diamond-shaped space, enclosing the bust of a man. The third pendant has two eagles, the crown of thorns, the pierced hands and feet, and the scourge. The lower room is entered by a trap from the upper, and is without ornamentation, one of its two windows being towards the tower, and the other towards the sea. The cave below is about 100 feet in length. The history of this tower is unknown.

CAIRNBULG.

THE Castle of Cairnbulg is situated in the parish of Rathen, on the bank of the water of Philorth, and about three quarters of a mile distant from the ocean. It is a ruin of considerable magnitude; and "consists of buildings of two periods. There is first the large oblong keep, which probably dates, at the earliest, from the end of the fifteenth century; and the buildings of a later date, which have been so contrived as to convert Cairnbulg into a castle with diagonally opposite towers, the old keep being made available as one of these towers."* The whole was in a habitable condition to the year 1785.

The lands of Cairnbulg, with its castle, formed part of the extensive domains of the Comyns, Earls of Buchan, and were confiscated in 1306, in consequence of the rivalry of that great family with the successful and chivalrous Robert the Bruce. The last earl of the name of Comyn died in England in 1329.

John Ross, son of the Earl of Ross, having married the daughter of Comyn, obtained from the crown a grant of half his territories, in which portion was comprehended Cairnbulg, but having no family by this marriage he disponed these lands by charter, dated at Inverness in 1316, to his brother, Hugh, Earl of Ross, and failing him, to Hugh, his second son, and Walter Leslie, who had married the eldest daughter. They were severally designated of Philorth until the year 1375, when that barony, including Cairnbulg, came into the possession of Sir Alexander Fraser of Cowie, by marriage with the youngest daughter and co-heiress of the earl, and the sister of Euphemia, Countess of Ross. By this marriage, Sir Alexander Fraser acquired the valuable estates of Philorth, Aberdour, and others in the counties of Aberdeen and Banff. After the forfeiture of the Comyns, the earldom of Buchan was bestowed upon Alexander Stewart, Lord of Badenoch, fourth son of Robert the second. He married the Countess of Ross, and died in 1394. The Frasers for two centuries seem to have made Cairnbulg their principal residence, but whether the square tower of the castle, certainly the most ancient part of the building, was erected by the Earls of Buchan or Ross, or by the Frasers after it came into their possession, it is now impossible to ascertain. The other portions of the castle were built by Sir

---

* MacGibbon and Ross—"Castellated and Domestic Architecture of Scotland," *Vol. I., p. 309.*

Alexander Fraser, the eleventh laird of that family, about the year 1545. His grandson and successor sold, in 1619, the lands and Castle of Cairnbulg to Andrew Fraser of Stonywood, father of the first Lord Fraser of Muchalls. This was the Sir Alexander who erected the castle on Kinnaird's Head, which became his residence, and where he died in 1623.

Spalding, in his History of the Troubles in Scotland in the year 1644, mentions the Castle of Cairnbulg on two occasions, in connexion with its then proprietor, the Lord Fraser of Muchalls, a strenuous Covenanter.

In 1703, Charles, the last Lord Fraser, sold the castle and estate to Colonel John Buchan of Auchmacoy; and, in 1739, it became by purchase, the property of Alexander Aberdein, whose son, in 1775, again sold it to the third Earl of Aberdeen, who, at his death in 1801, left it to his son, John Gordon, at whose death, in 1862, the estate became the property of John Duthie, who died in 1872, and was succeeded by his brother, William Duthie, Esq., the present proprietor.

XXIV.

KNOCKHALL.

KNOCKHALL, an ancient residence of the Udny family, is situated near Newburgh, in the parish of Foveran, and but a short distance removed from the southern bank of the estuary of the river Ythan. It was erected in 1565.

The lairds of Udny were Anti-Covenanters, and in 1639 the place of Knockhall was taken by the Earl of Erroll and Earl Marischal, with the lands of Delgaty and Ludquharn, on the part of the Covenant; and its capture, as was usual in similar cases, attended with spoliation and annoyance. In the following year, a foraging party, marching from Aberdeen, again assailed Knockhall; and, the laird being absent, they met with no resistance, the Lady Udny giving them free access to the castle. In 1644 the Lord Gordon came to Knockhall, on his route to Moray in search of his father. During this journey an event occurred very characteristic of the times. Meeting, in his transit through the county of Banff, one of the collectors of taxes, Gordon compelled him to advance the sum of two thousand merks; and encountering another collector, of the name of Geddes, he levied a contribution upon him of one thousand merks of the public money, and this under pretence of paying himself for levies he had raised in Banffshire.

The castle of Knockhall was, in the year 1734, accidentally burned; and has since continued in a state of ruin.

Knockhall Castle

XXV.

LEITH-HALL.

LEITH-HALL is situated in the parish of Kenethmont (originally "Kil-Alcmund," *i.e.*, the cell or chapel of Alcmund, a well-known saint in the Romish calendar), at the western extremity of the district of Garioch. It was, until altered by modern improvement, one of those massive towers, flanked by turrets, which appear to have been, in the close of the sixteenth and during the period of the seventeenth century, the peculiar style of architecture adopted by the lairds of Aberdeenshire. It was, in its earlier days, defended by a strong wall, having a turret at each angle, and containing an area of about two acres. Westward runs the river Bogie, from whose left bank rises the hill of Noth, on the summit of which is the most remarkable specimen of a vitrified fort, alike as to altitude, extent of area, or preservation, extant in Great Britain.

The name of Leith is of great antiquity in Scotland, and is evidently taken from the lands on which the town of that name now stands, which were originally a part of the barony of Restalrig, where there is evidence to show that the Leiths were seated at an early period.

The Leiths of Edingarroch—the head of the family, and now represented by that of Leith-Hall—were settled in Aberdeenshire in the reign of Alexander the Third, at which period Sir Norman Lesly, progenitor of the Earls of Rothes, married a daughter of the laird of Edingarroch. The immediate ancestor of the Leiths of Leith-Hall, was William Leith of Barns, a person of rank and distinction in the reign of David Bruce. He was provost of Aberdeen in 1350; and is said to have married a daughter of Donald, twelfth Earl of Mar. In 1358 he went to England as one of the hostages for the ransom of David, King of Scotland.

The house of Leith-Hall was built by James Leith, the thirteenth in succession, about the year 1650. His son, John Leith, married Janet, daughter of George, second Lord Banff, by Agnes Falconer, daughter of Alexander, first Lord Halkerton.

He died in 1736, and was succeeded by his son, who married Harriet Stewart of Auchluncart, by whom he had three sons: John who died unmarried in 1778; Alexander who succeeded, in 1789, to his grand-uncle, Andrew Hay of Rannes, and, on the death of his brother, to the estates of Leith-Hall and others. Alexander became a general in the army in 1813; and died on the tenth of May, 1838. James, his younger brother, who married the Lady Augusta Forbes, daughter of the Earl of Granard, was created a Grand Cross of the Bath, for distinguished services during the Peninsular War; he was also a Knight Commander of the Portugese Order of the Tower and Sword, a Grand Cordon of the Order of Military Merit of France, a lieutenant-general in the army; and died at Barbadoes on the sixteenth October, 1816, being then governor of that colony, and commander of the forces in the Windward and Leeward Islands. General Alexander Leith-Hay was succeeded by his son, Sir Andrew Leith-Hay of Rannes and Leith-Hall, who also served with distinction in the Peninsular War, receiving a medal and six clasps for general actions. He was a member of Lord Melbourne's administration, and represented the Elgin burghs, 1833-38, resigning on being appointed governor of Bermuda. He died in 1862, and was succeeded by his eldest son, Colonel Alexander Sebastian Leith-Hay, C.B., the present proprietor. The estates of the family have been obtained at different periods, commencing about the year 1300.

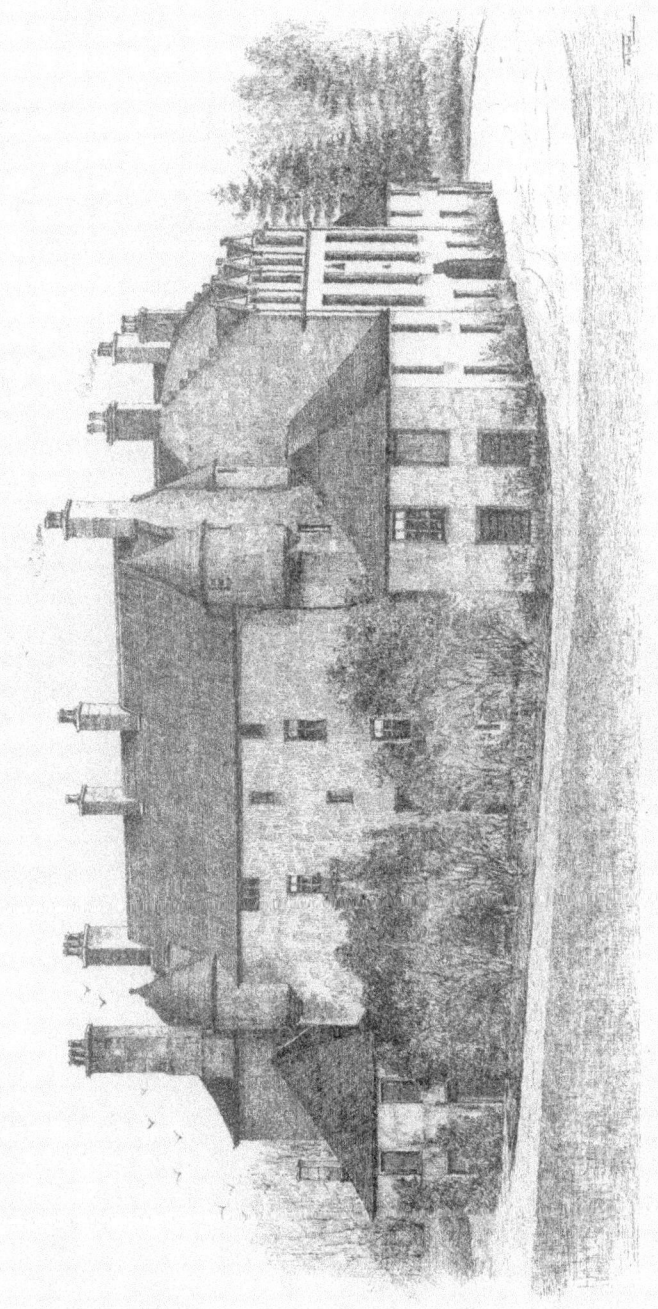

Leith-Hall

XXVI.

LESLIE.

LESLIE Castle is situated on the north bank of the Gadie, and in the parish of Leslie, which gave its name to the numerous and distinguished family of Leslie, or Leslyn, who possessed estates in the district as early as the twelfth century. The present castle was built in 1661, and has been one of the most commodious residences of its class in the county. Enclosed by a rampart and fosse, it was also, to the west, defended by a watchtower and drawbridge. Over the gateway is the date 1663; and above the entrance the inscription, "Hœc Corp. Sydera Mentem."

The first on record of the progenitors of the family, which took its name from the lands of Lesslyn, or Leslie, are named in a charter of those lands, granted by David, Earl of Huntingdon (1171-99), brother of King David I., "to Malcolm the son of Bartolf"—in which the granter announces his gift "clericis et laicis . Francis et Anglis . Flamingis . et Scotis . tam presentibus quam futuris". (The name of Bartolf stamps its bearer as of Teutonic race.) The next on record is Norman, "constabularius de Inverurin," where there was a castle of the Earls of Huntingdon and Garioch—wherein he is called son of Malcolm—who has a charter from Earl John (1219-37) of the lands of Lesselyn and Auchnagart. His son, Alforn (?—"Alformis" in the charter), also called "constabularius," had a charter from Alexander II. in 1248, "at the instance of Isobyle de Bruiss and her son, Robert de Bruiss, of his [Alforn's] lands of Lesselyn and his wood of Lesselyn, as he had hitherto held it in free forest." It is to be remarked that, although in possession of Lesselyn for now four generations, Alforn does not call himself anything but "son of Norman." The first who assumed a surname from the lands was his son, Sir Norman of Lesselyn, who swore allegiance to Edward I. at Aberdeen, 15th July, 1296. Fourth in descent from Sir Norman was David of Lesselyn, who, by his wife, a daughter of Provost Robert Davidson—killed at Harlaw—had an only daughter,

Margaret, who, marrying a kinsman, Alexander Leslie, a younger son of Sir Andrew of Balquhain, transmitted the name of Leslie of that ilk to their posterity; although the position of the family became less important, a large part of the estates, other than Leslie proper, having gone by settlement to the next principal branch, the Leslies of Rothes.

In the fifth generation from Alexander and Margaret, Lesselyn, or Leslie, fell to their representative, George Leslie, who married the daughter of Patrick, Lord Lindores; she surviving him, married John Forbes, son of the laird of Monymusk, by Lady Margaret Douglas, daughter of William, Earl of Angus. This John Forbes, from his lady's jointure, purchased up the debts on the estate, and became the possessor of the barony, and the first of the Forbesses lairds of Leslie. From Patrick Leith he bought Edingarroch and Licklyhead. His property of Durris, on Deeside, was plundered by the Royalists during the "Troubles"; and he was himself concerned in the burning of Pitcaple castle in 1645, and the release of Andrew Cant and Alexander Jaffray, his son being one of the leaders in that affair. John Forbes died shortly afterwards, and the barony passed to his son, William, who married Janet, sister of Lord Duffus. He re-built the castle of Leslie; and died in the year 1670. Their son, John Forbes, succeeded to the estate which, during his lifetime, became by purchase the property of the family of Leith-Hall, in whose possession it has since continued. This family had previously obtained the barony of New Leslie; and John, the ninth in succession, resided there, as did his son, James, until he erected the house of Leith-Hall, about the year 1650.

The remains of the castle of New Leslie have been eradicated by the progress of agricultural improvement; but its neighbouring stronghold, although in a state of ruin, exhibits, in the perfect state of its roofless walls, the substantial masonry of its construction, and from the road to Aberdeen, which passes in its immediate vicinity, presents an interesting specimen of the baronial castles of the seventeenth century.

The castle and adjacent lands form part of the Rannes estate, and are now possessed by the eighteenth proprietor, in direct succession from the Leiths of Edingarroch.

It may be mentioned that of the numerous branches thrown off by the house of Leslie, the only ones connected with Aberdeenshire, which are represented at this day in the male line, are the Leslies of Wardhouse and their cadets, the Leslies of Warthill.

XXVII.
LICKLYHEAD.

LICKLYHEAD is one of the old castellated houses of the early part of the seventeenth century. It is situated in the parish of Premnay, and on the right bank of the Gadie. It was erected in 1629 by Forbes of Leslie, who had recently purchased the estate from Patrick Leith of Edingarroch, an ancestor of the family of Leith Hall. The date of the erection, with the initials of John Forbes and his wife, are inscribed over the door. The tower is three storeys high; and on the turrets are some fine specimens of the cable ornament.

Henry Leith of Barns possessed Licklyhead in 1490. His last successor by inheritance, Patrick Leith, was served heir to his grandfather, William Leith, in 1620. The sale of Licklyhead to Forbes of Leslie took place in 1625.

In the year 1644, one of those events occurred so frequent in these troublous times, and which, being recorded, indicate very distinctly the dreadful state of society within the range of the unfortunate territories where a civil war was raging on the side of Royalty or of the Covenant. It is related by Spalding, that upon the night of Saturday the 17th August, Alexander Irvine of Kingcausie, on his route to Aberdeen, was met by William Forbes, natural son to John Forbes of Leslie, who happened to be coming out of that town on his way to Banchory, where his father then resided. This meeting took place about the Craibstane. Forbes, anxious to gain the reward of 5000 merks which had been offered by the Estates for the laird of Kingcausie, attempted to arrest him. The laird, spurning the idea of being the prisoner of a person he considered so much beneath him, refused to surrender; but during the parley Forbes drew a pistol from his belt, and, before Kingcausie could arm himself, shot him dead. Instead of being tried and executed for this murder, he was esteemed to have done good service. All that could be alleged against Kingcausie was that, accompanied by the young laird of Drum, he had visited Montrose.

William Forbes afterwards resided at Licklyhead, where, in August, 1645, firing a gun he shot off his hand; this, honest Spalding believes to have been a judgment against him, and relates that the right hand with which he shot the laird of Kingcausie, was the one carried away by the above accident. The laird of Leslie and of Licklyhead, in these days, was a zealous Covenanter; and much engaged in the contests resulting from the religious disputes which then oppressed and depopulated Scotland. In 1645, the Marquis of Montrose, carrying fire and sword into the Earl Marischal's country, burned the place of Urie, then the property of John Forbes of Leslie. Forbes, however, continued in arms; and, accompanied by the Earl Marischal, Viscount Frendraught, Lord Fraser, and other barons, came to Aberdeen on the 7th April, for the purpose of levying contributions on its inhabitants. They were interrupted in their proceedings by receiving intelligence that the Lord Gordon, despatched by Montrose, was in their immediate neighbourhood. Lord Gordon, with his brother, Lord Lewis, at the head of one hundred and sixty cavalry with a proportion of infantry, crossed the Dee, on the 8th of April, at Mill of Dinnet. This movement occasioned an immediate break up in the enemy's camp. Lord Marischal betook himself with all speed to the fastness of Dunnottar; and his companions separated without delay.

In the year 1692, the Forbesses of Leslie still possessed Licklyhead; but in 1701 Walter Hay became the proprietor; and in 1723 the estate was purchased by Patrick Duff, of the family of Craigston. It was afterwards sold to Thomas Gordon, who again disposed of it to Elizabeth Ogilvie; she married Rear-Admiral John Maitland, by whom it was again sold to Henry Lumsden of Auchindoir. In the year 1876 this old tower was completely restored and renovated in excellent taste, by the present proprietor, Hugh G. Lumsden, Esq. of Auchindoir, who succeeded his grandfather, the late Henry Lumsden of Auchindoir, in 1859.

Inchbrae Castle

XXVIII.
MELDRUM.

THE family of Meldrum is of great antiquity, the present proprietor representing the Meldrums, the Setons, and the Urquharts, who have, at different periods possessed the Barony, which, in all probability, gave a name to the parish in which it is situated.

Philip de Fedarg, a distinguished man in the reign of Alexander II., was knighted, and having disputed boundaries with the Abbot of Arbroath, their differences were finally adjusted on the 3rd August, 1236; the Abbot subsequently granting him, for his homage and services, the territory of Auchineve. It is uncertain whether this Philip or his son relinquished the designation of Fedarg, and assumed that of Melgdrum, but this happened in the reign of Alexander III., about the year 1249.

Sir Philip de Melgdrum, son of the above-mentioned Philip de Fedarg, married Agnes Comyn, sister of Alexander, Earl of Buchan. The dispute with the Abbot of Arbroath appears to have been hereditary, for Sir Philip and his lady contested the right of presentation to the church of Butkilny with that ecclesiastic, and the difference was terminated by a decision of the Bishop of Aberdeen, dated at Inverurie, in February, 1262. Sir Philip died in the end of the reign of Alexander III., and was succeeded by his eldest son, Sir William de Melgdrum, who espoused the cause of John Baliol, in his competition for the crown of Scotland, in 1291 and 1292. He was succeeded by his eldest son, John, of whose history nothing remarkable is recorded; he left two sons, of whom Sir Philip became his heir. His second son, William, became one of the ambassadors nominated to negotiate the liberty of David, king of Scotland, in 1348; he was ancestor of the Meldrums of Fyvie. Sir Philip was a steady supporter of King David Bruce; he fought bravely in the battle of Halidon-hill. He appears to have been much about the person of the king, and witnessed, among others, the charters creating Sir Malcolm Fleming, Earl of

Wigton, dated in 1341, and that to Sir Archibald Campbell, of Lochow, ancestor of the Dukes of Argyll, dated at Aberdeen in 1343. This brave knight was killed at the battle of Durham in 1346.

Sir Thomas de Meldrum, who succeeded him, was never married, and resigned the estates in favour of his brother, William, who obtained from David Bruce, a charter confirming to him and to his heirs, the lands and barony of Meldrum; this confirmation is dated in October, 1353. Sir William was succeeded by his only son, William, who also left an only son, who became the last male descendant of the Meldrums of Meldrum; he left two daughters, the eldest of whom, Mariotta de Meldrum, died unmarried, but his second daughter, Elizabeth, married William Seton, younger son of Sir Alexander Seton, Lord of Gordon, brother of Alexander, first Earl of Huntly, who, in right of his wife, inherited the barony of Meldrum, but retained his own paternal name, and became the first of the Setons of Meldrum. He was killed in the battle of Brechin, in May, 1452, leaving an only son, Alexander, who was served heir to his mother. He married Muriella Sutherland, by whom he had a son and daughter; this son was put in possession of the estate in his father's lifetime, and obtained a charter of the lands of Balcairn in 1490. Alexander, the fourth Seton of Meldrum, and son of the former laird, married Agnes, daughter of Patrick Gordon, of Haddo, ancestor of the Earls of Aberdeen, and by her had two sons, William, and Alexander, who was chancellor of Aberdeen; he married, secondly, Janet, daughter and co-heiress of George Leith of Barns. He was succeeded by his eldest son, William, who married, first, Janet, daughter of James Gordon of Lesmoir, and, secondly, Margaret, daughter of Innes of Leuchars; by the former he had three sons, and by the latter two. In January, 1556, charters were granted to Alexander, his eldest son, by which the succession to heirs general, as hitherto in force, was confirmed. This Alexander Seton married the daughter of the laird of Drum, by whom he had one son, Alexander. He married, secondly, Jane, daughter of Alexander Lord Abernethy of Saltoun, by whom he had several children. In 1584 he obtained a charter of confirmation under the Great Seal, whereby the future succession was to be in heirs male. By this means, his eldest son having predeceased him leaving an only daughter, his eldest son by the second marriage inherited the estate, and became the seventh laird of the name of Seton. He married Lady Grisel Stewart, and, dying without issue, was succeeded by his brother, William, who obtained by charter, dated July 10th, 1623, the estate of Balbithan. He married Anne, the daughter of James Crichton of Frendraught, ancestor of Viscount Frendraught; by this lady he had no family. Taking into

Meldon Castle.

consideration the long period during which the succession had been vested in heirs general, that the estate had come to his family by a female, and that it was fair and just that the course of succession should be restored to heirs general, he, therefore, in 1635, executed an entail of his whole estate in favour of Elizabeth, the daughter of his eldest brother, and, dying soon after, she came into possession, having married in 1610, John Urquhart, the tutor of Cromarty, by whom she had several children. Her eldest son, Patrick, succeeded her in the Barony of Meldrum, and became the first laird of the name of Urquhart. The antiquity of this surname is undoubted. The Urquharts of Cromarty, have always been considered the chiefs of the name, and in the 13th century had considerable property in the county of Aberdeen. Patrick, the ninth laird of Cromarty, and the first Urquhart of Meldrum, was born in 1611. He obtained by charter the lands of Forglen in Banffshire. He was a loyal supporter of Charles I. and suffered many losses and privations from his adherence to the crown; his house of Lethenty, which he held in property previous to his succession to Meldrum, was plundered by the Covenanters. Patrick married the Lady Margaret Ogilvy, daughter of the Earl of Airlie, a lady rendered famous by her having assisted her brother, Lord Ogilvy, in making his escape from the prison of St. Andrews, the night before he was to have been executed, in 1646. This she effected by disguising him in her own apparel, as has been subsequently successfully practised by the Countess of Nithsdale, in 1716, and by Madame de Lavalette, after the second restoration of the Bourbons, in 1815. Patrick, laird of Meldrum, died in 1664, and was succeeded by his son, Adam, who was for many years representative in Parliament for the county of Aberdeen; he married the Lady Mary Gordon, daughter of Lewis, Marquis of Huntly, and the sister of George, first Duke of Gordon. Dying at Edinburgh, the 10th November, 1684, he was succeeded by his son, John, who married Jane, daughter of Sir Hugh Campbell, of Calder, by Lady Henrietta Stuart, daughter of James, fifth Earl of Moray, by whom he had two sons and four daughters. During the reign of Queen Anne, he held the office of Master of Works in Scotland, in conjunction with John Campbell, of Mamore, whose son became Duke of Argyll. Dying at Aberdeen in 1726, his son, William, inherited the estate; and, on the death of Colonel James Urquhart, in 1741, he became the male representative of the Urquharts of Cromarty. William married, first, Mary, daughter of Sir William Forbes of Monymusk; secondly, the daughter of a merchant in Aberdeen; and, thirdly, the daughter of George Douglas of Whiterigs. William, his eldest son, entered the army, and died unmarried, in the twenty-first year of his age; his second son, Keith, became laird of Meldrum. He married Lady Jane Duff, eldest daughter of Lord Braco, afterwards Earl of Fife, by whom he had two sons and two daughters. James, his eldest son, succeeded him in his estates. He became an advocate at the Scottish bar, was a person of great private worth and considerable learning. He was for many years Sheriff of the county of Banff. The Sheriff was succeeded by Beauchamp Colclough Urquhart, of Meldrum and Byth, grandson of William Urquhart by his third marriage, who greatly added to and improved the old family mansion, ornamenting the grounds which surround it, and rendering it a residence worthy of the ancient family to whom it has for many centuries appertained. He was succeeded in 1861 by his eldest son, Beauchamp Colclough Urquhart, Esq., the present proprietor.

XXIX.

MIDMAR.

ON the northern slope of the Hill of Fare, and not far from the scene of the battle of Corrichie, is situated Midmar castle, which has been described in Billing's " Baronial and Ecclesiastical Antiquities of Scotland" as "one of the most picturesque and fanciful of the turreted mansions of Scotland;" and a recent writer in a pleasantly written paper thus refers to it—

"But not all the old houses and long-ruined towers have histories or names attached to them; there are some about whom even tradition is silent; but which, by their age, their rude architecture, or their isolated position, suggest a history so long past as to be forgotten. One such I can recall, as I look over yonder low line of hills, and picture to myself the quaint old house standing at the entrance of the wild glen which runs deep into the heart of the hill at its back; and I can think of none so solitary in its position, so complete in its character: yet I am told that very little is known of its history, or of its original owners, only that it has changed hands repeatedly in the last hundred years, and that it might once have been a hunting-lodge of the kings of Scotland.

"It has its low arched doorways, and small deep-set windows, its flagged court, and steps leading down to the garden. Deep shadows and strong lights lie upon it; a dashing burn flows down the glen, dark with over-shadowing trees; and above all, it has its green, secluded garden, where grow old-fashioned flowers, and where there are holes in the sunny wall for the beehives.

"In the garden is to be found, among others, a white rose, which, at anyrate there, is called the Jacobite rose; and its cream-white glistening petals, semi-double, with a circle of yellow stamens at its heart, may well have suggested the white cockade of satin, tied with a golden thread." *

When or by whom Midmar castle was built is not known. The lands would appear to have been in the possession of Adam Brown (of the Brouns of Fordell)

---

* "On a Hill-Top"—*Blackwood's Magazine*, September, 1886.

sometime in the thirteenth century. He was killed at the battle of Falkirk in 1298; and the estate, which he held of the bishop of Aberdeen, descended to his grandson, Sir John Brown, sheriff of the county of Aberdeen (1328), who was succeeded by his son, John, ancestor of George Brown, bishop of Dunkeld (1484-1514).

In the Acts of the Scottish Parliament, mention is made of a dispute between John Brown of Midmar and Robert D'Umfraville, both of whom were required to find bail for five hundred pounds Scots to keep the peace. The importance of the disputants is shown by the fact that the Earl of Mar became security for the one and Lord Keith for the other. John Brown, grandson of the sheriff, sold Midmar in 1422 to Patrick Ogilvy. In 1484 the first Earl of Huntly granted part of Midmar to his second son, Alexander Gordon, on whom James III. bestowed the lands of Abergeldie.

In 1593, during the conflict between the Roman Catholic and Protestant parties, the castle was burned; and it is supposed that the older part of the present structure was erected soon after that date. James Gordon is designed of Midmar in 1621.

Not only has Midmar castle frequently changed hands, but even its name has been repeatedly altered. In the seventeenth century it was known as Ballogie, and in the latter part of that century it was in the possession of Alexander Forbes, a descendant of the Forbeses of Tolquhon, who was a commissioner of supply for Aberdeenshire in 1678, and to whom the lands and barony of Midmar were ratified in 1681. Before 1732 the property had passed into the possession of a laird named Grant, who, in the hope of founding a family, had superseded the designation "Ballogie" by that of "Grantfield." In 1741 Alexander Grant of Grantfield was appointed sheriff-principal of Aberdeenshire, in succession to the Earl of Rothes; and he continued in office until 1748, when David Dalrymple, advocate, Edinburgh, afterwards Lord Westhall, was appointed.

In 1782 Midmar (again so named) had passed into the hands of an heiress, Margaret Davidson, only child of William Davidson, merchant in Aberdeen and provost of the city (1760-62), whose wife was a daughter of Burnett of Elrick. Miss Davidson married, in 1790, James Dalrymple Horn Elphinstone of Logie-Elphinstone, who had a sister married to James Mansfield, banker in Edinburgh, and partner of the firm of Bell & Rannie, wine merchants, Leith. About 1795 Mr. Mansfield became purchaser of the estate of Midmar. He died at Midmar castle in 1828, after having devoted himself with great perseverance to the improvement of the property. His son, John Mansfield, senior partner in the house of Bell & Rannie, succeeded him; at whose death the estate fell to his four

daughters, who, to carry out certain family arrangements, sold it to Colonel Gordon of Cluny in 1842.

The building bears evidence of having been erected in the sixteenth and seventeenth centuries; but one feature, that of the small paved court and steps leading up to it, so precisely resembles the same design at Castle Grant, that it is difficult to resist the conclusion that they were the work of the same architect, and belong to the same period—the early years of the eighteenth century.

XXX.
MONYMUSK.

MONYMUSK is situated in the parish of that name, near the site of its ancient priory, which, according to the tradition preserved by Hector Boece, was founded by Malcolm Canmore when proceeding on a military expedition against the people of Moray. The barony of Monymusk belonged to the crown, and was dedicated to St. Andrew and made over to the Bishop of St. Andrews in order to procure victory in the expedition.

The house, or castle, dates from the Reformation. Duncan, the son of William Forbes of Corsindae, obtained possession of the estate in 1549, and his son, William Forbes, employed the materials of the priory in the construction of the mansion, which has been added to by later proprietors, and now forms a spacious baronial residence. Surrounded by an extensive park, through which flows the river Don, it is sheltered by trees of great age and growth, and the plantations, extending for miles, are terminated by the picturesque and rocky summit of Benachie.

Duncan Forbes obtained a charter under the great seal, addressed to "Duncan Forbes de Monymusk," which is dated 1st December, 1554. He died in the year 1587, and was succeeded by his eldest son, William, who married Margaret Douglas, daughter of Sir William Douglas of Kemnay, who, in 1588, became the ninth Earl of Angus. Their son, William Forbes of Monymusk, married Elizabeth Wishart, daughter to the Laird of Pittarrow, and held charters of Portlethen and the barony of Torry. He was by patent, dated April 2, 1626, created a Baronet of Nova Scotia by Charles I. Sir William suffered many misfortunes on account of his steady attachment to the royal cause. His son, William, became the second baronet of Monymusk, and having married Jane, daughter of Sir Thomas Burnett of Leys, left one son and one daughter. Sir John, his heir, married Margaret, daughter of the Viscount Arbuthnott. By this marriage he had two sons and a

daughter. The eldest, William, succeeded to the title and estate in 1702, becoming the fourth baronet. He married Lady Jane Keith, eldest daughter of the first Earl of Kintore, and resided in Pitfichie Castle, now a picturesque ruin, which had recently passed from the Hurries into the possession of the Forbeses of Monymusk. Their elder son, John, who married Mary, daughter of John, Lord Pitsligo, died before his father, leaving two sons, the eldest of whom succeeded his grandfather, and became Sir William Forbes, the fifth baronet. He was Professor of Civil Law in King's College, Aberdeen, and father of Sir William Forbes of Pitsligo, the celebrated banker.

In 1712 the estate of Monymusk was purchased from Sir William Forbes, the fourth baronet, by Sir Francis Grant of Cullen, who was son of Grant of Ballentombe, a younger branch of the Grants of Grant. He had been created a baronet by Queen Anne in 1705, and in the following year was appointed a Senator of the College of Justice under the title of Lord Cullen. The price was £120,000 Scots, and Lord Cullen ruefully recorded that by bad advice he had purchased the estate by the sale of a better, namely, the baronies of Cullen, Doun, and Eden, in Banffshire. Monymusk was then in a very unimproved condition, and the people had a destitute and miserable lot. Lord Cullen at once set about making the best of his newly acquired possessions. It was in 1719 that the beautiful grounds of Paradise were laid out, prior to which time these grounds, and a considerable tract afterwards planted, were let as a farm at a rent of fifty shillings a year. At a great expenditure of labour Lord Cullen cleared and trenched the ground and formed a landscape garden which well deserved the name applied to it (which was taken from that of a neighbouring homestead thus curiously named), and planted in it the trees, which, in the course of years, have grown into the magnificent proportions that are the admiration of all visitors to Paradise.

Lord Cullen's successor, Sir Archibald Grant, born in 1696, and a man of great energy and enterprise, planted over fifty million trees on the estate, thereby adding to its value a great deal more than the price at which it had been acquired. Sir Archibald was also the pioneer of agricultural improvement. He represented Aberdeenshire in parliament from 1722 to 1731. William Grant, the second son of Lord Cullen, was also a distinguished lawyer—Solicitor-General for Scotland in 1737, Lord Advocate in 1738, raised to the bench in 1754 by the title of Lord Prestongrange, and afterwards Lord Justice Clerk. The successor of Sir Archibald Grant was his son, Archibald, who had been a captain in the East India Company's service, and who died in 1796. A third Sir Archibald Grant was his successor (born

1760, died 1820); three of whose sons were Sir James Grant, who succeeded him; Sir Isaac, the next in succession; and Mr. Robert Grant of Tillyfour, for many years convener of the county of Aberdeen. Sir Isaac was succeeded in 1863 by his nephew, Archibald, the 7th baronet, son of Robert Grant of Tillyfour, who, in 1886, was succeeded by his brother, Sir Francis William Grant, Bart., the present proprietor.

XXXI.

NEWE.

ON the north bank of the river Don, and added to the old mansion of the family, erected in 1604, stands the house of Newe, built in conformity to the wishes of his uncle, the late John Forbes of Bombay, by Sir Charles Forbes, Baronet, in the year 1831. The sum left by Mr. Forbes for this purpose has been judiciously expended, and the seat of his ancestors has become a spacious and elegant residence in the castellated style. The old house has been retained as a part of the building, which is of Kildrummy freestone, from a design by Archibald Simpson. To the north of the house rises the mountain of Ben Newe, and to the south is a lawn extending to the river.

Newe has for centuries been in the possession of the Forbeses. William, the first proprietor of that name, was designed "William of the Dauch," and was the younger brother of Alexander Forbes, third laird of Pitsligo. The family of Pitsligo is a branch of the noble family of Forbes, immediately descended from Sir John "of the black lip," whose eldest son, Alexander, became the first Lord Forbes; his second son, William, founding the Pitsligo family; the third, John, that of Tolquhon; while the fourth, Alister Cam, was the progenitor of the Forbeses of Brux. William became Sir William Forbes of Kynaldie, and married Agnes Fraser, the daughter of Fraser of Philorth, and by this alliance obtained, in 1424, from his father-in-law, the lands and barony of Pitsligo. He died about the year 1446, and was succeeded by his son, Sir Alexander Forbes of Kynaldie and Pitsligo, who married a daughter of the Earl of Erroll; their eldest son, William, acquired the lands of Lethenty and Meikle Wardes in the Garioch, and married Marion, daughter of Sir John Ogilvie, of Lintrathen. William Forbes died before his father, leaving two sons, Alexander and William, the former becoming, on the death of his grandfather, in 1477, the heir of the Pitsligo line, and the latter, "William of the Dauch," as above-mentioned, the ancestor of the family of Newe. The Pitsligo family thus diverged into two branches, and towards the close of the fifteenth century, the direct representation was carried forward by the elder of these, while from the younger descended the house of Newe. The death of the master of Pitsligo, in 1781, terminated the line of the elder branch in direct succession from Alexander Forbes of Pitsligo; and Sir Charles Forbes of Newe, as the direct heir male and lineal descendant of "William of the Dauch," the brother of Alexander, was, in the year 1833, by a jury, before the Sheriff of Aberdeenshire, of which General Hay of Rannes was the chancellor or chairman, served heir male of Alexander Lord Forbes of Pitsligo, the father of the last lord, who was attainted for having joined the standard of Prince Charles Edward, in 1745. John Forbes of Newe, who died in 1751, married a daughter of Arthur Forbes of Brux, and was succeeded by his son, Captain John Forbes of Newe, late of the 42nd regiment or Royal Highlanders. He married a daughter of Colonel Grant of Ballindalloch, and left a son, Major John Forbes of Newe. Captain Forbes died at Castle Downie in 1775, and was buried in Lord Lovat's vault, in the church of Kirkhill. Major John Forbes married Miss Duff of Muirton, and they had an only child, afterwards Lady Grant of Monymusk. On his death, in the year 1792, without male issue, the family of Newe became represented by the Rev. George Forbes of Leochel, son of John Forbes of Bellabeg. A younger brother of the Rev. George Forbes was Mr. John Forbes, who established the great mercantile house of Forbes & Co., of Bombay. He purchased the estate of Newe, and began a system of great improvements in the district. Among his private benefactions was a gift of £10,000 to the lunatic asylum at Aberdeen, in the grounds of which there is a handsome obelisk to his memory. He entailed the estates of Newe, Bellabeg, &c., upon his nephew, Charles, son of the Rev. George Forbes, who was a member of the house of Forbes & Co., purchased Skellater and Corgarff from the Forbeses of Skellater, was created a baronet of the United Kingdom in 1823, and for twenty years represented Malmesbury in parliament.

John, the eldest son of Sir Charles Forbes, and heir to the families of Pitsligo and of Newe, died at Ventnor, in the Isle of Wight, in 1840, at the age of thirty-nine years, having been born at Bombay, on the 15th December, 1801. He was a director of the East India Company, and for some years one of the representatives in parliament for the Borough of Malmesbury, as his father's colleague. Mr. John Forbes married in 1828, the daughter of Henry Lanoy Hunter of Beach-hill, in the county of Berks, by whom he left a son, Charles, born 15th July, 1832, and four daughters. Sir Charles Forbes, the first baronet, died in 1849, and was succeeded by his grandson, Charles, who dying unmarried, in 1852, the title devolved on his

uncle, Charles Forbes, who became third baronet, and was succeeded in 1877 by his son, Sir Charles John Forbes, fourth baronet. His son, Sir Charles Stewart Forbes, succeeded in 1884.

XXXII.

PITCAPLE.

THE Castle of Pitcaple is situated on the southern bank of the river Ury, and in the parish of Chapel of Garioch. The precise date of its erection cannot now be ascertained, but, from its design, probably dates from early in the seventeenth century, although the lower part may be older. In itself composed of strong and massive masonry, it was also fortified by a lofty wall which surrounded the court-yard, beyond which was a fosse or moat, with a drawbridge communicating with the castle gate; the round tower and the pointed turret were the characteristic features of the building. In modern times the surrounding wall has been removed, the moat filled up, and all indication of the necessity of warlike preparation has entirely disappeared. The castle was renovated and added to about 1830 in conformity with its ancient architecture, and considerable additions have been made to it by the present proprietor. The principal tower at the north-east angle of the old castle was formerly designated the "Thane's tower."

Pitcaple formerly belonged to the Leslies, a branch of the ancient family of Balquhain. David, the first laird of the name, was the son of William, fourth laird of Balquhain, and obtained a charter of the lands of Harlaw, Ressivet, and barony of Pitcaple in 1447. He was succeeded by his brother, James, and married the daughter of Seton of Meldrum, by whom he had three sons, David, his heir, James of Ressivet, and Walter. The latter was parson of Monymusk. He married secondly Elizabeth Stuart, daughter to the Earl of Athol. By his first wife he had Robert, an advocate at the Scottish bar, who purchased part of the barony of Kinnaird. He died in 1537. Alexander, the fourth laird, married Margaret, daughter to Gordon of Achanassie, and was succeeded by his second son, George, who married Christian Leslie, daughter to Wardhouse. He unfortunately killed George Leith of Treefield, which exasperated the then numerous families bearing that name against him. He was a man of remarkable strength and undaunted courage, and although none of the Leiths

Heagle Castle

ventured singly to attack him, he was after many wanderings obliged to leave the country, and died in Germany a captain in the imperial army.

The dispute which occurred between Crichton of Frendraught and Gordon of Rothiemay led to disastrous consequences, and amongst others the often related burning of the house of Frendraught, in which strife James Leslie, second son to the laird of Pitcaple, was much implicated. The lands of these proprietors being adjacent, disputes as to right of property led to personal hatred, and of course, as was invariably the case in those licentious days, the friends of either party espousing the cause of the hostile barons, armed to support the pretensions of their respective champion. With others the above-mentioned James Leslie joined the Crichtons, and on the 1st January, 1630, they left Frendraught for Rothiemay, with the purpose either of making its owner their prisoner, or of insulting him by fierce defiance on his own territories. Information of this onslaught having been given to the laird of Rothiemay, he resolved to set forth and encounter his assailants, accompanied by his son, and a small party of horsemen and foot. Having crossed the river Deveron, his party soon encountered the Crichtons, and a serious conflict took place, which terminated in the defeat of the Rothiemay party. Considering the violence of feeling, and the nature of the encounters of those times, the loss of life appears to have been unusually small. The laird of Rothiemay died of his wounds, as did the brother of Gordon of Lesmore, while on the side of the Crichtons John Meldrum of Reidhill was the only person seriously wounded. John Gordon, the eldest son of the deceased laird, to revenge the death of his father, collected his followers, and assisted by the freebooter, James Grant, and his associates, he resolved to lay waste the lands of Frendraught, in which he had greater probability of success from the absence of Crichton, then in England, who lost no time in submitting his case to the king, and soliciting the interference of the law to check these violent and reckless proceedings. A Commission was in consequence issued by the Lords of the Council, empowering Frendraught and others to apprehend John Gordon and his associates. This delegation proving insufficient, the Council sent Sir Robert Gordon of Gordonstoun, tutor of Sutherland, and Sir William Seton of Killesmuir, to the north with fresh powers; and believing that additional influence would be requisite to produce an amicable settlement, and to quiet the district agitated by the warfare of these hostile barons, the Commissioners were instructed to solicit the aid of the Marquis of Huntly and the Earl of Moray, in their labours for the restoration of amity and peace.

The Commissioners lost no time in proceeding to the north, and having separated at Aberdeen, Sir Robert Gordon went to Strathbogie, but was disappointed in seeing the Marquis of Huntly, who had gone to attend the funeral of the laird of Drum.

On the day of Sir Robert's arrival at Strathbogie, the Grants, James and Alexander, descended from the mountains, with a party of two hundred Highlanders to join in the foray against the laird of Frendraught. The intervention of the Commissioner now became most important, and the results eminently successful. Having heard of the advance of the Grants, he immediately proceeded to Rothiemay, where he found John Gordon and his vassals armed and in the act of setting forward to meet their lawless associates. It so happened that the Earl of Sutherland, the nephew of Sir Robert, was then at Rothiemay on a visit, and joining him in persuasion, they not only induced John Gordon and his friends to desist from their intention, but prevailed upon James Grant to disperse his band, and retire to the wilds from whence he came.

Subsequently the Commissioners visited Huntly Castle, and, in conjunction with the Marquis, prevailed upon the hostile lairds to reconcile their differences, and refer all matters in dispute to their decision. The terms of this adjustment were agreed to by the parties, and they shook hands in apparent amity and reconciliation.

The laird of Frendraught had no sooner brought this serious quarrel to an end, than a dispute arose with the laird of Pitcaple. John Meldrum of Reidhill having been wounded in the scuffle where old Rothiemay lost his life, had been allowed some compensation by Frendraught in recompense of his partizanship; but Meldrum, conceiving this gratuity disproportioned to his own estimate of his services, thought abuse might induce Frendraught, particularly when accompanied with threats, to bestow upon him a more liberal allowance.

Frendraught continuing obstinate, Meldrum acted very much in the custom of the times, and without ceremony carried off two horses from the park, for which act he was prosecuted for theft, and refusing to appear, was declared rebel. Meldrum had taken refuge in the house of John Leslie of Pitcaple, whose sister he had married. As a Commissioner, Frendraught on the 27th September, 1630, went in search of Meldrum, and on the lands of Pitcaple he met with James Leslie, the second son of that family, and one of his former adherents in the skirmish with Rothiemay.

Instead of giving Frendraught assistance in the object of his visit, Leslie remonstrated with him, bringing to his recollection the services performed in his behalf by his brother-in-law, Meldrum, and himself, in his feud with Rothiemay. This seemed to soften the laird of Frendraught; but Robert Crichton of Conland became incensed at the freedom with which Leslie addressed his kinsman, and high words having passed, Conland drew a pistol from his belt and shot young Leslie in the arm, but with such effect that he was carried home apparently in a dying state.

This laid the foundation of the fearful tragedy, which events growing out of this quarrel tended to produce. The Leslies confederated and flew to arms, while Frendraught, apprehensive of the powerful attack he had every reason to anticipate, proceeded on the 5th October to solicit the intervention of the Marquis of Huntly, and also of the Earl of Moray. With the latter he was unsuccessful, but Lord Huntly agreed to mediate. Accordingly a messenger was despatched to Pitcaple requesting his attendance at Huntly's residence, the Bog of Gight. The laird learning that Frendraught was at The Bog, determined not to proceed there without an escort; but having assembled and equipped about thirty horsemen, he marched to the conference. Upon his arrival, as might naturally be expected, he complained bitterly of the injury which his son had sustained, declared his determination to be revenged, and declined to listen to any amicable adjustment until it was ascertained whether his son would survive the wound he had received. Irritated at the defence made by the marquis for Frendraught, Pitcaple mounted and abruptly left the castle with his followers. Hearing that the Leslies were assembled and watching the return of Frendraught, Lord Huntly detained him for two days, and would not then permit him to depart without an escort, ordered to see him home in safety. At the head of this party were John, Viscount Aboyne, and the laird of Rothiemay. They arrived without interruption at Frendraught, where they were hospitably received, and entreated to remain for the night. To this they unfortunately acceded, and the following dreadful occurrence took place:—The sleeping apartment of the Viscount was in the old tower of Frendraught, leading off from the hall; immediately below this apartment was a vault, wherein there was, according to Spalding, "ane round holl devised of old, just under Aboyne's bed." His page, English Will, as he was called, and Robert Gordon from Sutherland, slept in the same room. The laird of Rothiemay with some of his servants were in an upper chamber, immediately over that in which the Viscount slept; and in an apartment directly above the latter were laid George Chalmer of Noth, Captain Rollock, one of Frendraught's party, and George Gordon, servant to Aboyne. About midnight the whole tower almost instantaneously took fire, and so suddenly and furiously did the flames spread over and consume the edifice, that of its inmates the Viscount, the laird of Rothiemay, English Will, Colonel Ivat, a friend of Aboyne's, and two other persons, perished.

Robert Gordon, who lay in the same chamber with the Viscount, made his escape, as did George Chalmer and Captain Rollock. As Robert Gordon saved his life, it is probable that Lord Aboyne might also have done so, had he not resisted advice to get away as fast as possible, instead of which he ran to the chamber of Rothiemay and awakened him to his danger. While he was performing this friendly action, the staircase took fire, and cut them off from all means of retreat; they then appeared at a window looking to the court, calling for assistance, which in all probability it was impossible to afford them. Spalding, without explaining what possible effort under such circumstances could have saved the inmates at the summit of a tower enveloped in flames, with its narrow staircase and surrounding wood-work on fire, and filled with smoke, seems to reflect on the conduct of the family of Frendraught. He states, "The laird and the lady with their servants all seeing and hearing this woful crying, but made no help, nor manner of helping, which they perceiving, they cried oftentimes mercy at God's hands for their sins, syne clasped in other's arms, and cheirfully suffered this cruell martyrdome."

This mysterious and melancholy event was calculated to increase the heats and animosities then prevailing in the north of Scotland, and to occasion doubts and prejudices as to the authors of a conflagration which was considered as a wilful and premeditated act, and not the result of accident.

That Frendraught or his family were implicated in this atrocious act, does not appear to be within the range of probability. The Leslies were with more reason suspected, they and their adherents having not only threatened to burn the house of Frendraught, but had, as was proved before the Lords of Council, entered into negotiations to that effect with the notorious James Grant, the cousin-german of Pitcaple, whose lawless character induced them to select him as a fit instrument for such a purpose. The parties immediately employed in instigating Grant to commit this crime were John Meldrum of Reidhill, and Alexander, the brother of Pitcaple.

In consequence of a strong representation made to the Council by the Marquis of Huntly, the Bishops of Moray and Aberdeen, Lord Carnegie, and others, were ordered to investigate into the circumstances which occasioned the fire; and accordingly these personages were met on the 13th April, 1631, at Frendraught, by the Lords Gordon, Deskford, and Ogilvie, who proceeded to examine the ruined tower, and all parts of the building, to ascertain, if possible, the cause of the catastrophe. After diligent search they arrived at a conclusion that the conflagration could not have resulted from accident, that it was very improbable it could have been occasioned by any external application, and that it must have been raised by some means employed within the vaults or chambers of the tower; probably the latter, for it is unlikely that a fire lighted in one of the vaults, constructed as they were in those days, could have spread so rapidly over the whole building, as to have rendered escape in many cases impracticable.

Great suspicion attached to John Meldrum, who was apprehended and conveyed to Edinburgh, where he was afterwards tried, condemned, and executed. His conviction must have resulted more from the circumstances under which he was placed by his own quarrel with Frendraught, as well as his having warmly taken up that of his brother-in-law, James Leslie, than from any proof adduced of his having committed the act; and the evidence of two of James Grant's men, who swore to the fact of Meldrum having tampered with that rebel, wishing him to undertake the burning, must also have weighed against him; but great writers on the Criminal Law of Scotland have expressed doubts as to the guilt of Meldrum, or of the sufficiency of proof to have occasioned a verdict positively identifying him with the horrible crime for which he suffered. A prediction of Meldrum's expressed to Sir George Ogilvie of Banff, on the evening before the fire, was certainly presumptive evidence against him, namely, that "unless a reconciliation was immediately effected between him and the laird, it would never happen, as the house of Frendraught would be burned before morning." When brought out for execution, Meldrum to the last protested his innocence, although he fully admitted the conversation with Sir George Ogilvie.

Pitcaple being on the direct road from Aberdeen to the north, was in former times visited by many royal and distinguished personages. The gay and chivalrous monarch, James IV., when on a progress to repress the turbulent spirit of his barons, was one of its visitors, but he must have been received in an earlier building than the present. The unfortunate Mary Queen of Scots passed part of a day at Pitcaple on her way from Balquhain to Rothiemay, after hearing mass at "Our Lady's Chapel of the Garioch," where the parish church now stands. During her visit she is said to have breakfasted under a thorn tree, a portion of the trunk of which still remains. These were the visits of regal prosperity, but the arrival of the celebrated and noble Marquis of Montrose was marked by incidents calculated to awaken the deepest sympathy. Generals Leslie and Strachan, on their route south with Montrose as their prisoner, after the battle of Carbisdale, halted at Pitcaple—on which occasion the illustrious captive was mounted on a miserable highland pony, his feet being tied together by ropes, while before him rode a herald, who proclaimed, "Here comes James Graham, a traitor to his country!" The lady of Pitcaple, anxious to liberate her unfortunate guest, suggested to him a means of escape through a chimney-like shaft leading up and through the wall of his chamber, but the marquis replied that he "would rather take his chance in Edinburgh." He was hurried on to that city, and in a few weeks after was sentenced to death by the covenanters, and executed. The room in which he was confined at Pitcaple is still called Montrose's room.

In the month of July, 1650, Charles II. landed from Holland at Garmouth, from whence he proceeded to the Bog of Gight, and on his journey southward sent notice to the laird of Pitcaple that he intended to visit him. This rather astounding intimation was communicated to Mr. Leslie when attending the neighbouring market of "St. Sair's Fair," who without delay purchased all the claret in the market, and proceeded homewards to receive his royal visitor. When the royal party came in sight of the fair at some distance, and discried the tents pitched on the ground, they concluded that it must be an encampment of covenanters. To avoid the hazard of an encounter they quitted the high road for some distance. When Charles crossed the Ury near the castle of Pitcaple he was much struck with the luxuriance of the crops, observing that it reminded him of England. The farm was subsequently called England, which name it still retains. On the occasion of this royal visit a ball took place, the party dancing under and in the vicinity of Queen Mary's Thorn. On the following morning, when Charles took his departure from Pitcaple, the Duke of Buckingham was on his right hand, and Argyll on his left. In the assembled multitude to witness so rare a sight as a royal cortege was a shrewd old dame, familiarly known as the "Guidewife of Glack," who, nothing daunted either by the presence of Majesty or that of Argyll, exclaimed with a shrill voice, "God bless your Majesty, and send you to your ain; but they are on your left hand that helped to tak aff your father's head, and if you takna care they will hae aff yours next." These anecdotes were related by the late Miss Lumsden of Pitcaple, the great-grand-daughter of John Leslie, the laird who entertained the king, and afterwards accompanied him to England, where he was in the royal army at the battle of Worcester. The last laird of the Leslie family died in 1757, when the property fell to his sister, who married John Lumsden, Professor of Divinity in King's College, Aberdeen, by whose two daughters it was sold to Henry Lumsden, grandfather of the present proprietor, Henry Lumsden, Esq., of Pitcaple.

XXXIII.

RAVENSCRAIG.

THE Castle of Ravenscraig stands on a rocky eminence immediately on the southern bank of the river Ugie. It appears to have been built, though possibly on the foundations of an earlier stronghold, in 1491, in which year Gilbert Keith of Inverugie, and his wife, Jonete Grahame, had a charter from King James IV. of the superiority of the lands of Torterston, or Tortastoun, and others, and "the rocks commonly called *le Ravinnscraig*," with licence to build a castle or fortalice on the said rock, with drawbridge, portcullis, battlements, and all other necessary defences. Ravenscraig, or "the Craig of Inverugie," continued thereafter to be the head castle of the barony of Torterston, which was originally the property and residence of the Cheynes, a family of Anglo-Norman descent, that settled in Scotland in the earlier part of the thirteenth century.

In the year 1258, Reginald de Chene was one of the Scottish barons that concluded a treaty with the Welsh, and in 1267 he became Chamberlain of Scotland. In 1284, Reginald, with his son, of the same name, were among those who engaged to accept the Princess Margaret as their queen. They were present at the parliament held in 1291, and were jointly appointed the nominees of Baliol. Sir Reginald, the father, died soon after he had married Eustace, the heiress of Sir William Colville of Ochiltree, in Ayrshire, who outlived her husband, and having, in 1296, sworn allegiance to Edward the first, retained her lands in the shires of Ayr, Aberdeen, Banff, Inverness, Kincardine, and Forfar, which properties she had either succeeded to in heritage, or obtained in dower. Sir Reginald Chene, the son, became Sheriff of Inverness in 1292; he married Mary, the eldest daughter and co-heiress of Freskyn of Moray. As the eldest daughter, she inherited the castle and barony of Duffus, with other lands in Moray, Caithness, and West Lothian. Henry Cheyne, the second son of old Sir Reginald, was Bishop of Aberdeen, and, bending to the subjugation in which the first Edward appeared then to hold Scotland, he swore allegiance to that monarch.

In 1305, Sir Reginald Chene was appointed one of the Justiciaries in the north; he died previous to the year 1313, when Robert the first confirmed a convention entered into by Maria, the wife of the late Sir Reginald Chene, and Alexander Fraser of Philorth, the husband of Jane, the second daughter of William, Earl of Ross.

The son of Sir Reginald inherited the wide domains of his father, and was one of the Scottish barons who, in 1330, wrote a celebrated letter to the Pope. He was present at the battle of Halidon Hill, in 1333, where he was taken prisoner. Dying about the year 1350, he left two daughters, who inherited his estates. Mariot, the senior, married Sir John Douglas, by whom she had no family; and secondly, John of Keith, the second son of Edward of Keith, the Marischal of Scotland, by whom she had a son, Andrew, who succeeded to her estates. Mary married Nicol, the second son of Kenneth, Earl of Sutherland, who obtained with her the barony of Duffus; from this marriage descended the family of Sutherland, Lord Duffus. Thus ended the male line of the eldest branch of the Cheynes of Ravenscraig. The castle and estate then became the property, by female descent, of the family of Keith, for an account of which see the notes on "Inverugie." There is little known of the history of the castle during the sixteenth and seventeenth centuries, though we read that King James VI., during an expedition to the north, in 1589, visited The Craig of Inverugie, and was present at the marriage of a daughter of the then laird, who it will be noted, represented the male line of the Keiths of Torterstoun, or Ravenscraig, though the Earl Marischal, having married the daughter of the laird's elder brother, had acquired with her the superiority of the lands. It is not very clear when the younger branch, which thus possessed Ravenscraig, became extinct, but the property, with the castle, appears to have been forfeited by its superior, the last Earl Marischal, after the rising in 1715.

It is now the property of the Merchant Maiden's Hospital, a valuable charity connected with Peterhead.

Rosserais Castle

XXXIV.

TERPERSIE.

THE old castellated house of Terpersie, or Dalpersie, situated in the parish of Tullynessle, and in a valley nearly surrounded by the hill of Coreen, like many of the residences of the old Scottish lairds, is erected at the very extremity of the estate attached to it. It is about a mile to the westward of the old military road leading to Alford, which crosses the Suie hill from the north, but intervening high grounds prevent its being observed. Except to those proceeding to the farm, or to the sportsman who looks down from the grouse shooting grounds in its immediate vicinity, it is never seen by the traveller or the stranger, and is a most sequestered and retired abode. The building is not remarkable either for its architectural importance or its extent, but situated as above described, in the centre of heath-covered mountains, with some fine old trees, and a rapid and clear stream running past, it presents, when approached, a picturesque and interesting object. It was built in 1561, that date being on the oldest part. The design was simple but admirably adapted for defence. A square main-building was defended by two round towers (all still existing) placed at the diagonally opposite corners—each of which from its shot-holes commanded two sides of the square. In later times, however, an addition had been made which somewhat interferes with this arrangement; but it was still a strong "house of defence," though not of great size. It has a peculiarity in having the stairs which lead to the different stories entirely in the thickness of the wall.

William Gordon, of Terpersie, was the eighth son of James Gordon, of Lesmore, and his second wife, Margaret Ogilvy. He was at the battle of Corrichie, in 1563; and, in 1573, he was also present at the battle of Tillyangus, where he killed "Black Arthur," the brother of Lord Forbes. He was then under the orders of Adam Gordon, of Auchindown, whom he also accompanied at the battle of Craibstane, near Aberdeen. He built the house of Terpersie, and surrounded it with a moat, close on the march between his property and that of Lord Forbes. With the Earl of Huntly, and those under his orders at Corrichie, the laird of Terpersie was proscribed; he subsequently died in the house of Rannes, and his remains are deposited in Rannes' Aisle, in the parish church of Rathven.

William Gordon was succeeded by his son, George, who married Miss Ogilvie, of Inverquharitie. His eldest son, by that lady, married the daughter of Gordon of Leitcheston, and was succeeded by his second son, James, in the lands of Terpersie, his eldest, Alexander, having predeceased him, unmarried; James Gordon married Anne, the laird of Craig's sister, dying at Terpersie was interred, as his father had been, in the Church of Tullynessle. George Gordon, son of the former laird, became his successor, and married the sister of Sir Alexander Burnett, of Craigmile, by whom he had a son, Charles, who possessed the estate after his death. Patrick Gordon, of Badenscoth, married the daughter of Ogilvie, laird of Banff, by whom he had three sons and two daughters, the elder of whom married Gordon of Knockespock.

After the battle of Auldearn, the army of General Baillie was quartered in Cromar, and, alike doubtful as to the future movements of his defeated colleague, General Hurry, or those of the victorious Marquis of Montrose, he remained encamped for some time between the kirks of Tarland and Coull, plundering the estates in the neighbourhood, and, during that time, his troops burned the house of Terpersie.

After the battle of Culloden, the then laird of Terpersie, who had joined the army of Prince Charles, after continuing for some time a wanderer in the hills near to his house, was induced to revisit it. Information having been given, a party of soldiers surrounded the place, and, after diligent search, captured him in a concealed part of the building, from whence he was withdrawn, and speedily executed. His estate was forfeited, and, like many others similarly situated, came into the possession of the York Buildings Company. It was subsequently purchased by a descendant of the former family, James Gordon, who had been a successful merchant at St. Kitts, in the West Indies, and died in 1770. His brother, Colonel Henry Gordon, succeeded, and was followed (1787) by his son, Harry Gordon, of Knockespock, who died in 1837. The property then reverted to James Adam Bremner, great-grandson of the eldest sister of James Gordon of St. Kitts, and grandson of Mr. Whitbread, M.P., who assumed the name and arms of Gordon. He was the patron of William Thom, the Inverurie poet. On his death in 1854, without issue, the estates were inherited by Sir Henry Percy Gordon, great-grandson of the youngest sister of James Gordon, of St. Kitts. He died in 1876, and was succeeded by Hannah Gordon, daughter of Harry Gordon, the last proprietor of that name, and wife of Admiral Fellowes.

Terpersie Castle

XXXV.

TOLQUHON.

TOLQUHON, situated in the parish of Tarves, formerly belonged to the Prestons. Sir Henry Preston was a leading man in the latter part of the fourteenth century, and received from King Robert III., in 1390, a grant of the lands and baronies of Formartine, Fyvie, &c., on the resignation of Sir James Lindsay. He is supposed to have fought in the battle of Harlaw; and was still alive in 1413. On his death his lands were divided—Fyvie going to the eldest daughter, who had married a Meldrum; and Tolquhon to Marjorie, the second, who had been a widow and was now re-married (1420) to Sir John Forbes, brother of the first Lord Forbes. Thus was established the family of Forbeses of Tolquhon, a distinguished branch of the race from whence they sprung, having for their descendants the families of Culloden, Ballogie, Foveran, Waterton, &c. The first Forbes of Tolquhon was the third son of "Sir John with the black lip," and consequently, from his parentage, was the head of the family with the exception of the Lords Forbes and Pitsligo.

The tower, built by the Prestons, is the most ancient part of the building, which had been greatly added to by subsequent proprietors, forming a quadrangle, with an extensive court and a fine entrance gateway, between two defending towers. Tolquhon has the remains of a residence where, in addition to a building considerable in extent, though somewhat confused in design and not very interesting in its details, great pains have been taken to ornament the grounds. It is still sheltered by stately timber, and the garden and orchard appear to have been upon a scale worthy of the mansion. The horse chestnut, ash, and beech trees, while the castle and the decorative works of art are in a state of ruin and decay, present an appearance of health and luxuriant foliage strongly contrasting with the desolation they surround and adorn. An inscription on the front of the building proves the date of its construction, and is to the following effect :—

ALL . THIS . WARKE
EXCEP . THE . AVLD
TOVR . WAS . BEGVN
BE . WILLIAM . FORBES*
15 . APRILE . 1584
AND . ENDIT . BE . HIM
20 . OCTOBER . 1589.

The Forbeses continued to possess Tolquhon all through the "troubles" of the seventeenth century. Among the Tolquhon papers in the possession of Mr. Forbes Leith of Whitehaugh, is an autograph letter of Charles II., dated 14th June, 1651, forbidding any levy to be made on Tolquhon, as the laird, Walter Forbes, was more than sixty years of age, while his son, Alexander Forbes, was commanding a regiment. Alexander Forbes of Tolquhon not only fought bravely for Charles II. at Worcester, but assisted him in escaping from that fatal field; and having mounted the king on his own horse, continued to obstruct the pursuit of the enemy until disabled by a wound which left him prostrate amongst the dying and the dead, where he was found, still alive, on the following day. In 1653-54 he was knighted by the exiled monarch, and about the same time he received the freedom of the burgh of Haddington and the cities of St. Andrews and Glasgow. In 1649 he had married Bathia Murray of Blackbarony, widow of Sir William Forbes of Craigievar, whose zeal as a Covenanter was not less than that of her second husband as a Royalist. Sir Alexander died, without issue, in 1702.

William Forbes, the eleventh in succession, married Anne, the heiress of John Leith of Whitehaugh, and by her had two sons and a daughter. His predecessor, in the latter years of his life, had been subjected to the control of designing people; and being then in a state of dotage, he, under their guidance, so burdened the estate that a sale became necessary; at all events, the same parties that had brought on this state of affairs, procured its sale, which took place by order of the Court of Session in 1716, the purchaser being Lieutenant-Colonel Francis Farquhar, from whom it passed to William, Earl of Aberdeen. William Forbes was so dissatisfied with the transaction, and with the decision that had placed his paternal

---

* This William founded an hospital "for four poor men, who were to eat and lye here, and to have each a peck of meal, and three shillings, a penny, and two-sixths of a penny Scots, weekly; also some meal, peats, &c."—"*Collections for the Shires,*" p. 330.

estates in other hands, that he refused to quit the house until attacked by a detachment of troops in January, 1718, when he was wounded and made prisoner. He subsequently went abroad, but returned in 1728; and, dying the same year, was, on the tenth of April, buried in Westminster Abbey.* His son, William, studied at Oxford, and became successively curate of Binsay, near Oxford, and vicar of Thornbury, in Gloucestershire, at which latter place he died in September, 1761, without issue.

John Forbes Leith became, by his brother's death, the representative of the family of Tolquhon. He married, in 1743-44, Jean Morrison, eldest daughter of the laird of Bognie, by whom he had three sons. William Forbes Leith, the eldest, was born in 1748, and died unmarried in 1806. He was succeeded by his brother, Theodore, who studied medicine and settled at Greenwich as a physician. Upon his brother's death he became resident at Whitehaugh, where he died, in August, 1819, from the consequences of an accident.

His elder brother having died young, James John Forbes Leith succeeded his father. He had early in life gone to India as an officer in the service of the East India Company, and retired with the rank of lieutenant-colonel. He married on the twenty-eighth November, 1827, Williamina, only daughter of Lieutenant-Colonel James Stewart, of the Forty-second Royal Highlanders. Dying in 1843, Colonel Forbes Leith was succeeded by his eldest son, James, whose successor (1875) was the Rev. William Forbes Leith, the present owner of Whitehaugh.

Tolquhon, with the adjoining estates, are now the property of the Earl of Aberdeen.

* "The fortunes of the house, like those of many another Scottish family, were probably consumed by the fever of the Darien scheme, in which Alexander Forbes of Tolquhon appears to have embarked beyond his means, the stock he held (£500) having been judicially attached."—Billing's "*Baronial and Ecclesiastical Antiquities of Scotland.*"

XXXVI.

TOWIE.

THE old Castle of Towie, of which the ruins of one tower alone remain, is seated on an eminence, at the base of which runs the river Don, there a precipitous and rapid stream. It was built by the Forbeses of Brux, and came into the possession of their collateral descendants.

William Forbes of Towie was the son of William Forbes of Little Kildrummie; his son, Alexander, who succeeded him, married Christian Barclay, daughter of the laird of Towie Barclay, by whom he had one daughter. He married, secondly, Janet, daughter of Patrick Gordon of Haddo, who became the mother of Alexander Forbes of Towie, in whose time the fearful tragedy connected with the castle was enacted.

It has been a disputed point whether the burning of the family of the laird, recorded by many authorities, took place at Towie or Corgarff. Mr. Matthew Lumsden evidently confuses the fact. He states that John Forbes of Towie, married, first, the daughter of John Grant of Ballindalloch, by whom he had a son, "who was unmercifully murdered in the castle of Corgarffe." He proceeds to state that after the death of his first wife he married Margaret Campbell, daughter of Sir John Campbell of Calder. Other authorities state that the lady so barbarously treated was this Margaret Campbell, but that she was the wife of John's son, Alexander, which disproves Mr. Lumsden's assertion, that the son of the first marriage was murdered in the castle of Corgarff, or that this murder, if it did occur, had any connection with the circumstances detailed in the ballad, and leaves no doubt that Towie was the scene of the events therein recorded. Archbishop Spottiswood informs us that, "anno 1571, in the north parts of Scotland, Adam Gordon (who was deputy for his brother, the Earl of Huntly) did keep a great stir, and, under colour of the Queen's authority, committed divers oppressions, especially

upon the Forbeses, having killed Arthur Forbes, brother to the Lord Forbes. Not long after he sent to summon the house of Tavoy (Towie) pertaining to Alexander Forbes. The lady refusing to yield without direction from her husband, he put fire into it, and burnt her therein, with children and servants, being twenty-seven persons in all. This inhuman and barbarous cruelty made his name odious, and stained all his former doings, otherwise he was held very active and fortunate in his enterprises."

Doctor Percy thinks that the name of Ker is assumed, and substituted for Gordon, in the narrative of this catastrophe, but that there is no doubt Adam Gordon, of Auchindown, was the hero of the ballad; and he also states that the minstrels of the age substituted names to suit their hearers, and consequently imputed the barbarity here deplored, to a Gordon or a Ker, as answered their purpose.

Buchanan, in his history of Scotland, records the fact, that the Castle of Towie, with Lady Forbes and her whole household, thirty-seven in number, was burnt by Adam Gordon, brother to Lord Huntly.

This barbarous act exasperated the Forbeses, who mustered under the master, and their pursuit of Adam Gordon terminated in the conflict at the Craibstane, near Aberdeen, between the Gordons and the Forbeses, in November, 1571.

Alexander Forbes died in 1580, and was succeeded by the second son of his marriage, after the above events, with the daughter of John Forbes of Reires; this son married Elizabeth, daughter of Duncan Forbes of Monymusk; their son, John, succeeded his father, and married Margaret, daughter of John Sumner of Brodie, by whom he had two sons, Alexander and Arthur, called Black Arthur of Towie. In the person of this Alexander, the regular succession of the house of Towie failed. In 1684, the castle and estate belonged to Arthur Forbes of Brux; to him succeeded Roderick, the possessor, in 1696. Arthur Forbes obtained the estate in 1717, and in 1726 it was sold to Arthur Gordon of Carnousie; in 1745 it became the property of Alexander Leith of Freefield; in 1808 it was purchased by Sir Harry Niven Lumsden, and became the property of Henry Lumsden of Auchindoir. The present proprietor, Hugh G. Lumsden, Esq., of Auchindoir, succeeded his grandfather, the late Henry Lumsden of Auchindoir, in 1859.

XXXVII.

TOWIE BARCLAY.

THE Castle of Towie Barclay is situated in the parish of Auchterless, close to the great road leading from Fyvie to Turriff. The building is very ancient, and, although in architectural beauty no longer conspicuous, it deserves a place in this work, not only for its former merits, but in consideration of its having been the property and residence of one of the oldest families in the county. The venerable structure continued in a tolerably entire state until about the year 1792, when Mr. Irvine, the then tenant, took off the roof, removed the turrets and embrasures, and razed two stories from its height, placing upon the dilapidated castle a vulgar modern roof; he also filled up the fosse, which constituted the only remaining feature of former baronial consequence.

"This demolition is the more deeply to be regretted, because the portions of the castle still standing, consisting of a range of vaults, and above, part of the principal floor of the main tower, are altogether of earlier date, and much superior in execution to the generality of the castles in North Britain. Of those vaults little can be said as they present merely the ordinary semicircular stone arch; but very different is the groined room above them forming the subject matter of our illustration. We may in some measure account for this superiority by stating that this apartment is indeed, both in its general design and carefully finished detail, more like a chapel than a baron's hall. Its ribbed groining, and the minor details, mark it as decidedly the work of an ecclesiastical architect, acting for a proprietor deeply imbued with religious sentiment, for, excepting the foliated detail of the brackets carrying the great ribs, the whole ornament has reference to sacred emblems. Indeed, the whole architecture of this room has a religious tone; and were it not for the existence of the great fireplace at the opposite end of the gallery, and for the small heavily-barred windows, both of which mark its real character as a baron's hall, we should fancy ourselves within a small church. It may possibly at times have served for both purposes; and here we leave the question, merely stating that in its style and execution we are strongly impressed with its affinity to the ecclesiastical architecture of the middle of the fifteenth century. Within the walls of the keep-tower there is, on the principal floor, the great hall, thirty feet long, and twenty feet in width, and at the end is the small staircase, *the closet-room*, and an unusually large principal circular stair immediately in connection with the central doorway. The entrance to the gallery at the end of the hall is most unusual, being from a *descending* staircase in the thickness of the wall, commencing from the floor above." *

Not many years ago the incongruous slated roof, that had been put over the walls, was removed and the present bartizan erected.

Among the Saxon followers of Margaret, the sister of Edgar Atheling, and Queen of Malcolm Caenmore, came to Scotland John Berkeley, descended from the English family of that name, and flying from the persecution which followed the Norman conquest. Hume states that Malcolm, "partly with a view of strengthening his kingdom by the accession of so many strangers, partly in hopes of employing them against the growing power of William, gave great countenance to all the English exiles. Many of them settled there, and laid the foundation of families which afterwards made a figure in that country." Of these, John Berkeley obtained the lands of Towie, in Aberdeenshire. His eldest son married the heiress of Gartly, by which he became possessed of a considerable estate; and his second son inherited the lands of Towie.

In the reign of William the Lion, there were four eminent men in Scotland of the name of Berkeley or Barclaie, sprung from the same stock, and united by consanguinity, namely, Walter, William, Humphry, and Robert. The two first were Great Chamberlains of the kingdom. Walter is so designated, in a donation granted by him to the monks of Aberbrothock, of the church of Inverkeillor, in the county of Forfar, which was confirmed by William the Lion; and William is also designated Chamberlain, in a charter granted by the same monarch, to the Friars of the Cistertian order. Walter de Berkeley was one of the hostages for William the Lion to Henry II. of England. He was appointed Chamberlain in 1165, and returned to Scotland with his sovereign, about the year 1174. It appears, by charter of confirmation from William the Lion, that Walter de Berkeley of Inverkeillor, was contemporary with, and cousin-german to, Humphry, the son

---

* Billing's "*Baronial and Ecclesiastical Antiquities of Scotland.*"

of Theobald de Berkeley, the progenitor of the family of Mathers, in the county of Kincardine.

Alexander was the name of the founder of the family of Tollie. At what time he acquired the estate does not appear, but he died in 1136; he might therefore be son of Walter, above referred to, and the constant recurrence of that name in the family is noteworthy, for, during the whole 617 years the barony was in their possession, Walter and Peter were alternately the name of the lairds, with but four exceptions, namely, one Alexander (the founder), two Johns, and one William. It is also probable that this Alexander was ancestor of the Barons of Gartly. The disputed point as to the chieftainship being whether the eldest son was called Walter after his grandfather, or Alexander after his father.

The antiquity of the castle is proved by the following inscription on its walls :—

Sir Alexander Barclay of Tolly, foundator, decessit A.D. 1136.

And on the same stone is carved—

P   In tim of valth, all men sims frendly,
          An frind is not knawin but in adversitie—1593.

Higher up the building, on a scroll, appears—

Sir Valter Barclay, foundet Tollie Miles, 1210.

There were other inscriptions, which are now removed or obliterated.

The first charters of the estate were carried off by Edward I. of England. In the roll of missing charters, in the reign of Robert Bruce, is "Carta to Walter Berkley de Kerko, Burgess of Perth," over the lands of Tollie. Robert granted a like charter, dated first August, 1322, in the sixteenth year of his reign.

About the year 1385, Andrew Berkeley, laird of Garutellie (Gartley) gave "the lands of Melrose, with the Mill, to Janet de Berkeley, widow of Sir John, of Monymous, Knight," in quittance of certain lands of her father, John Berkeley. Among the witnesses to this charter is William Berkeley of Tollie. This estate of Melrose, with Cullen, in Buchan, remained in the family for upwards of three hundred years; they also possessed Drumwhindle, and other lands about Ellon, as also at one time, Fintry and Craigfintry, in the parish of Ken-edar, now King Edward, and were a very powerful family previous to, and long after, the reign of Robert I.

In the metrical legends of the achievements of Sir William Wallace, the names of "the Berkeley," "the Bisset," and "the Boyd," are of constant occurrence, as his companions in arms. With their relative, David, Earl of Huntingdon and Garioch, the Barclays led their followers to one of the crusades, for them a disastrous expedition, the tradition being, that they carried five hundred followers with them, and returned with ten! It appears uncertain whether this is the occasion mentioned by Ariosto, but the probability is that the Barclays made more than one crusade to the Holy Land; and the following extract shews that they at one time accompanied the Earls of March and Richmond:—

> "Vidi il Marchese de Barclei, e appresso
> Di Marchia il Conte, e il Conte de Ritmonda
> Il primo porta in beanco un monte fesso
> L'altero la palma il terso un pin vell-onda."
>
> *Orlando Furioso*, canto x., sta. 80.

The barons of Gartly were the hereditary high sheriffs of Banffshire; on the coast of which, about Banff, they had large estates; and, although situated in Aberdeenshire, the barony of Gartly was, by their request, made a part and portion of the county of Banff, to which it still appertains. The Tollie family held the same office in Aberdeenshire, but for a short period, for, on the usurpation of Edward the first, Norman Leslie became the high sheriff of that county. After the Soulis conspiracy, and the black parliament of Scone, in 1320, among those accused of treason, was "Valterus de Barclay, Vicomes, Aberdone Miles;" and for this crime, David de Berkeley, Lord of Brechin, nephew to the king, lost his head. Buchanan mentions this circumstance, and laments his loss as a young man of great promise, who had taken no part in the conspiracy, and had only concealed his knowledge of it, in consequence of his being made acquainted with the fact under an oath of secrecy.

Between the Tollie and Gartly families, the closest intimacy and alliance, cemented by at least one intermarriage, appears to have existed. The marriage alluded to, produced important changes in the relative position of the families. The following account of it, is taken from M'Pherson's preface to Wyntoun's "Cronikyl of Scotland":—

"The royal manuscript marked 17.DXX, which is greatly superior to all the other manuscripts of Wyntoun known to exist, appears to have been transcribed for George Barclay of Auchroddie, and very soon after, the autograph of the corrected copy. Several good judges of manuscript, have pronounced it to be of the beginning of the fifteenth century. At the top of the page, in large characters, is the following—

> "This buik dois perteine
> To ane rycht honorabill man,
> George Barclay of Auchroddie,
> And mony wther propirty.
> Brother-german is he
> To Schyr Patrik of Tollie,
> Cheif of Barclays, in Scotland,
> And mony guid deid he's had in hand.

> "Schyr Patrik Barclay of Tollie,
> Cheif of that name, I testifie,
> As in his scheild ye may sie,
> Tua corsis weiris he,
> The thrid be resone quhy
> That hous marit properlie,
> Ane dochter of Gartlie,
> With gryt honor and dignitie,
> Quhilk than wes Barclay,
> An was ane Knyght ryght worthy," &c.

By this marriage with the heiress of Gartly, the properties became united, but did not long continue so, the eldest son succeeding to the estate and honours of Gartly, and the second becoming Laird of Tollie. In the reign of Mary, both families were warm partizans of that unfortunate princess; they shared in all the plots of the time, and, among others, joined heart and hand with the Earls of Huntly and Errol, in their rebellions against the Regent; and a Colonel Barclay, who resided in Spain, conducted the negotiations with that court, in what was called "the Spanish plot." In consequence, on the suppression of this imprudent rebellion, their estates were seized, and the males of the race, of any consequence, were obliged to take refuge in France and Spain. It is to this period that the inscription, "In time of valth," &c., refers, and not to the erection of the castle, which, from its style, evidently belongs to the thirteenth or fourteenth centuries.

> "Tollie Barclay of the glen,
> Happy to the maids, but never to the men,"

is said to have been the weird of Thomas the Rhymer to the lords of this now ruinous stronghold.

Among other males of the family who were compelled to consult their safety by immediate flight, was William Barclay, a very accomplished young man, an eminent scholar, and who had been secretary to the queen; he sought and obtained protection at the court of Lorraine. Having paid his addresses to a young lady of the court, he was informed that, previous to a marriage taking place, he must prove his descent from an ancient and noble family. Accordingly, application was made to James the sixth, and, in the edition published at Leyden, in 1659, of Barclay's "Argenis" there is the copy of a letter from that monarch to the Duke of Lorraine, dated 19th March, 1582, bearing testimony to the high birth and honourable affinities of William Barclay. The certificate is most ample, and bears that it was granted at the request of the Earl of Huntly and several other persons of high rank, and, amongst them, "Valtero Barclay, Domino et Barone de Tollie."

John Barclay, the author of the "Argenis" and other works, was a man of learning and genius, but of great eccentricity. He was intended for the church, which he never could be induced to enter, and, instead of becoming a clergyman, in his celebrated work, he published the severest satires against the Priests and Jesuits ever written since the days of Juvenal; neither would he join the Reformed or Protestant Church, in consequence of which, he made himself obnoxious to both. He died at Rome, leaving a large family. One of his sons went with the French Ambassador to Sweden, ultimately married in that country, and settled in Livonia, which subsequently became a province of Russia. His great-grandson entered the Russian service when very young, and, being a man of talent and enterprise, he rose rapidly in rank. In 1806, he was a general officer, commanding a division of the Russian army sent to the assistance of Prussia against the Emperor Napoleon; he was present at the battle of Wagram, and had a horse shot under him at Eylau, where he was also severely wounded. His services on these occasions so raised him in the estimation of the Emperor Alexander, that he appointed him minister-at-war, created him a prince of the empire, and gave him the baton of a field-marshal.

At the commencement of the celebrated campaign of 1812, he was placed in the chief command of the Russian army, and became the adviser of the emperor, to the jealousy and dislike of the ancient Russian noblesse. To him is attributed the plan of resistance to be adopted in that ever memorable campaign, namely, removing the people, and leaving the country desolate through which the French army was to pass. It is well known that, following up his original plan, Barclay de Tollie, after fighting a battle at Smolensko, continued his retreat, which added to the displeasure of the Russian nobility, and, notwithstanding his sound reasoning in defence of the line of conduct he had adopted, his removal from the command took place; and Kutusoff, probably to avert the same fate which had resulted to his predecessor, fought and lost the battle of Borodino. The Emperor Alexander did not withdraw his confidence from Marshal Barclay, but continued him in office as minister-at-war, and brought him with him to London in 1814.

From 1558 to 1624 there is no investure of the estate. It was then held by Patrick Barclay, whose initials are given to the moral reflection over the entrance, "In time of valth," &c.

The next investure is to Walter Barclay, as heir male to Patrick, who is designed "Fiar" of Towie. Walter died in 1636. His son, Patrick, is retoured as heir male to his father in 1643. In 1668 William Barclay was served heir to Patrick. He held the estate in trust for Elizabeth Barclay, who married John Barclay, or Gordon, of Rothiemay; and on the third February, 1693, a charter was granted to the said Elizabeth Barclay, designed lady of Towie, and John Gordon, her husband, in life-rent; and to Patrick Barclay, their only son, whom, failing the other heirs male of Elizabeth, then to her heirs female. These are followed by sasines, which conclude twenty-fourth September, 1713. Patrick had one son who proved fatuous, and a daughter who married Sir Alexander Innes of Coxtown, and by him had one daughter, Isabel, who married the Honourable Charles Maitland, brother to the Earl of Lauderdale. Isabel succeeded to the estate on the death of her brother, and it was sold by Mr. Maitland in 1753.

The weird, "Happy to the maids but never to the men," was said to follow the family in the death of the heir male who seldom survived his father; and so strong a hold had this in the belief of the people, that it was by them assigned as the reason for the sale of the estate in 1753. It was then purchased for £10,000 by the Earl of Findlater, for his second son, who died a few years after and when little more than of age. His death was considered another verification of the prediction of Thomas the Rhymer; and Lord Findlater, one of the ablest men of his day, was so far from being above the current superstition, that ever after, on his journeys to and from the south, when arriving upon the estate, at either boundary, he closed the blinds of his carriage until he passed the fated territory. In 1792 he sold the estate, for £21,000, to the trustees of Robert Gordon's Hospital (now College), in Aberdeen. It was during the Earl of Findlater's ownership that the turrets and battlements were taken down.

The late Sir Robert Barclay, K.C.B., a distinguished officer in the service of the East India Company, was a cadet of the Towie family. He received, in 1816, an augmentation to his arms, in commemoration of his services at the battle of "Assaye."

Robert Barclay, author of the Apology for the Quakers, was born at Gordonston, in the county of Moray, on the twenty-third December, 1648. His ancestors are traced back, by unquestionable documents, to Theobald de Berkeley who lived in the reign of David I. of Scotland. David came to the throne in 1124, and was consequently the contemporary of Henry I. of England, son of William the Conqueror.

Alexander de Berkeley, the fourth in succession from Theobald, having obtained by marriage, in 1351, the lands of Mathers, the family afterwards became designated by the appellation of De Berkeley of Mathers, until his great-grandson, also named Alexander, changed the patronymic to the present mode of spelling Barclay. The eighth in descent from Alexander Barclay was David, who sold his paternal estate of Mathers after it had remained for centuries in the family. The designation of Mathers was consequently lost; and in 1648, on the purchase of Ury by David, son of the last Barclay of Mathers and father of Robert, the family assumed that of Ury. This David Barclay of Ury, commonly called Colonel Barclay, was born at Kirtonhill, the seat of the Barclays of Mathers, in 1610. Early in life he became a volunteer in the army of Gustavus Adolphus, in which he rose to the rank of major. On the breaking out of the civil wars he returned home, and became colonel of a regiment of horse in the royal army; but on the success of Cromwell in Scotland he lost his military employment, which he never subsequently resumed. In 1647 he married Catherine, the daughter of Sir William Gordon of Gordonston. In requital of his attachment to the royal cause he was, after the restoration, committed a prisoner to the castle of Edinburgh, from whence he was liberated without any charge having been brought against him. In this prison he met with John Swinton who is said to have converted him to the religious principles of the Society of Friends, but he did not profess them openly until some years after.

Robert, the celebrated apologist, studied at the Scotch College in Paris, of which his uncle (son of the last Robert Barclay of Mathers) was then the rector. After publishing various works, he died on the third October, 1690.

Gartly, so often mentioned in the above notice, is in the last state of ruin and dilapidation: its mouldering walls have been assailed for the purpose of obtaining the materials for building and other purposes; but the tough old masonry has resisted with a tenacity occasioning some doubt, in the minds of the operators, as to the expediency of wasting time and misapplying labour in tearing it to pieces.

The Gartly family are said to have resided at one period chiefly in the castle of Banff, near to which town they had large estates. By the published "Poll Book of Aberdeenshire," we find that Mountcoffer belonged to them, which, although situated in the immediate vicinity of Banff, is in the county of Aberdeen. This appears to have been an acquisition of later date than when they were the hereditary sheriffs of the former county, and had the barony of Gartly transferred from Aberdeenshire.

There is a tradition that the Barclays led the van of the king's army in one of the numerous rebellions in the north, and that, in an action fought in Ross-shire, the chief of their name slew the rebel leader in single combat, for which he was rewarded by the grant of a considerable estate near Tain; and this is so far confirmed that to this day several families in Easter Ross bear the name of Barclay, in a country almost exclusively peopled by the Rosses and the Munroes.

The sketch of Towie Barclay is taken from a sepia drawing by Colonel Ross-King of Tertowie.

XXXVIII.

UDNY.

THE old tower of Udny, as it stood before the present extensive additions were attached to it, was an unusually fine specimen of the square "peel tower," as such are called in the southern parts of Scotland. Standing up, as it did, in a somewhat bare country, which was only broken by some rows of old beeches, along roads and fences at some distance from the castle, it was a striking object, and seen from a considerable distance.

There is no record of the date at which the castle was built, but, from some details in the architecture, it is evidently not later than the fifteenth century. Its plan is very simple, being an oblong, "forty-six feet in length outside; inside, twenty-eight feet; breadth outside, thirty-five feet; inside, seventeen feet; height, seventy-one feet. The walls are thick enough to have bed-closets within them. The two under stories are vaulted, the upper one of which contains a spacious hall, the whole length and breadth of the castle . . . Its height to the crown of the arch is about twenty feet." There is a tradition that the castle was built by three different lairds, who each raised it a story. It may be so, as life was precarious in the middle ages, but they had, successively, only carried out the original plan, which was that of a very perfect building of its kind.

There had no doubt been a courtyard, with "laigh-building" round part of it, as was invariably the case with a residence of the rank of Udny; but our immediate ancestors seem to have had an antipathy to such adjuncts to their dwellings, as they have, with very few exceptions, been swept away. They were, however, possibly, in many cases, little convenient according to more modern ideas, and, perhaps, ruinous besides. One interesting feature in the old castle was a spring of beautifully pure water, just inside the entrance door, the well being in a recess in the wall. It has of late years been built over, but, no doubt, still exists "in situ."

The estate of Udny has been for many centuries in possession of a family bearing the same name, which was, undoubtedly, assumed from it. The first proprietor whose name occurs in our records is "Patrick of Uldeny" (as it was then spelt), who died before 1406. Surnames were not, however, assumed from lands, for the first time in a family, at so late a date as that. The forefathers of this Patrick must have possessed "Uldeny" a full century earlier. The fourth proprietor on record (apparently a grandson of Patrick) is mentioned as "Dominus," or baron of Uldeny, in 1469. Five generations later, the family after having fallen on evil times and become deeply involved in wadsets and other unpleasantnesses, was, fortunately, rescued and placed in a better position than ever before by the success of two brothers, John and Robert Udny, in their career as merchants in Amsterdam. They were successively proprietors of Udny, the second, John, coming to the estate on his brother's death. He largely increased the property; purchased the barony of Belhelvie; the barony of Newburgh, with its mansion-house of Knockhall; and the lands of Fiddes and Monkshill. He married Isabel Fraser, by whom he had four sons and one daughter. The descendants of his eldest son, Alexander Udny, became extinct in the male line three generations afterwards, and the succession to Udny opened to the descendants of John Udny's second son, Robert Udny of Auchterellon, after an interval, during which the estate was possessed by the descendants of the heir-female, they being a branch of the Frasers of Philorth.

This Robert Udny had married Elizabeth, only daughter of Colonel John Fullarton of Dudwick, and died in 1708. He left two sons, Alexander, who died in 1712 without issue, and John, who succeeded to his maternal grandfather in the baronies of Birness and Dudwick, for which he took the name of Fullarton, and to his father in Auchterellon. This last-named estate he sold. He married Mary, daughter of Sir David Falconer of Newton, Lord President, sister of David, fifth Lord Falconer of Halkerton, and had three sons, 1st, John Fullarton of Dudwick, who married Mary, daughter of Sir John Guthrie of King-Edward, without issue. (He was "out in the '45," and was exempted from the benefit of the Act of Indemnity afterwards.) 2nd, Robert (Udny) Fullarton, who succeeded his brother in Dudwick, &c., was a general in the Russian Service, and Knight of the Order of St. Catherine of Russia. He died unmarried in 1786. 3rd, James Udny, advocate in Aberdeen, who married Jane, daughter of Alexander Walker, provost of that city, by his wife, Helen Irvine of Drum, and died in 1761. His eldest surviving son, Robert, succeeded, as mentioned further on, to Udny, &c.; his second, John, H.B.M's Consul at Venice and at Leghorn, married, in 1777, Selina, daughter of John Cleveland, Esq., M.P., Secretary to the

Admiralty, and died in 1800, leaving—besides a daughter, Julia, who married, in 1804, William Richard Hamilton, of the family of Belhaven, H.B.M. Minister at Naples, and sometime Under-Secretary for Foreign Affairs—a son, John Robert Udny, who eventually succeeded to the estates.

The elder son, Robert Udny above mentioned, F.R.S. and F.A.S., was a merchant in London. He was born in 1722, and succeeded to the family estates of Dudwick on the death of his cousin, General Fullarton, in 1786, and to that of Udny in 1792, on the death of the heir of line, William Fraser Udny. He married, 1st, Miss Hougham (whose sister was wife of the eighth Earl of Northampton), and 2nd, Margaret Jourdan, sub-governess to the Princess Charlotte. He died in 1802, leaving an only daughter, Mary, married, in 1785, to Sir William Cunningham of Milncraig, Bart.

Mr. Fullarton Udny was succeeded in the estates, under their entail, by his nephew, the above-named John Robert Udny, who was born at Leghorn in 1779. He attained the rank of colonel in the Coldstream Guards, in which regiment he saw a good deal of service. Colonel Udny married, 1st, Emily, daughter of Thomas Fitzhugh, Esq., of Plas Powen, co: of Denbigh, by whom he had one son, John Augustus Udny, born 1817, who died, a colonel in the Coldstream Guards, unmarried; and, 2ndly, Ann, daughter of David Allat, Esq., by whom he left one son, John Henry Fullarton Udny, who, on the death of his father, Colonel Udny, succeeded to the estates of Udny, Dudwick, and Newburgh, and to the representation of this ancient family.*

Mr. Udny married, July 8th, 1874, Amy Camilla, daughter of Sir John George Tollemache Sinclair, Bart., of Ulbster, county of Caithness. He has fitted up and added considerably to the old castle, which had for many years been uninhabited, rendering it a spacious and handsome residence. Also, while taking advantage of what old timber time and neglect had spared, he has laid out extensive policies round it with much taste. The plantations, which already shelter and beautify the grounds, only require a few more years to make Udny fit to compare favourably with many places which have not suffered from the non-residence of their proprietors, nor from the dilapidation which, under such circumstances, is the inevitable consequence.

* These details of the history of the Udny family are principally drawn from information supplied by the Rev. William Temple, St. Margaret's, Forgue, whose genealogical collections on the families seated in the district of Formartine are both extensive, and valuable from their accuracy.

XXXIX.

WESTHALL.

WESTHALL, situated in the parish of Oyne, stands looking towards Benachie, on a high and finely timbered plateau, which, falling away in front, slopes gradually down to the Gadie. There is no record of the date at which the house was built, nor by whom. Judging from its style and details, the early part of the 16th, or, possibly, the later years of the century before, may not be far from the truth. It had originally consisted of a double square tower, arranged in the common "L shape," with a rounded projection in the angle between them, resting on a moulding and containing a small turnpike-stair, which communicates only between the first and second stories. Apparently the communication between the ground-floor (which, as usual, is vaulted) and the latter had been by a ladder—a not uncommon arrangement in the smaller of our old "houses of defence."

The round tower, rising from the ground at the south-east corner of the building, which, later, contained the principal staircase, was added, most probably, in the 17th century, when some additions were made to the house. The entrance was then arranged to come through the tower, the door opening on the foot of the staircase. Although very small, and somewhat rudely built, Westhall was a complete little fortalice. It is, probably, the smallest example of its class which has regular open bartizans crowning its towers. A courtyard, with gateway and outbuildings, was only removed within the last fifty years—but the little old castle stands very much as it did—the extensive additions, which have been made at various times, fortunately being so attached to it as not to interfere with the integrity of the original building.

Westhall does not seem to have been very long the property of any one family, but to have passed, at comparatively short intervals, from one owner to another.

In 1451 we find it in possession of Edward Ramsay, who had lately acquired it from John Malwile (Melvile) of Hervistoun. "From Ramsay" (we read in the

"Antiquities of the Shires of Aberdeen and Banff, p. 441, *Note*), "the lands passed to Ingeram, Bishop of Aberdeen, in 1454. The Bishop granted them in the same year to a chaplain, celebrating the usual religious services for the souls of the founder; and of the King [James II.]; of his Queen; and of David Lindesay, second Earl of Crawford,—in the cathedral church of Aberdeen." In 1544, "William Abbircromye," eldest son and heir of "Jacobus Abbyrcrommye de Petmathen," receives a grant of "the feu-ferm of Westhall." In 1549, Mr. Lawrence Young pays "10 merks of cess for his lands of Westhall." In 1589, "Mr. Walter Gordon of Westhall" is mentioned. In 1649-50, "James Gordon of Westhall" was Collector of cess. The Abercrombies, however, had either recovered, or had in some way kept up their right of property in the lands, as, in 1681, Sir Alexander Abercrombie of Birkenbog sold Petmedden and Westhall to the Rev. James Horne, vicar of Elgin, who settled there, he having "demitted" his living at the Revolution, rather than take the test, or give in his adhesion to King William. Mr. Horne married Isabel, daughter of John Leslie, seventh laird of Pitcaple, by his wife, Agnes Ramsay of Balmain; by whom he had a son, John, and two daughters,—Isabel, married, in 1688, to Robert Douglas of Bridgefoord; and Agnes, who married, in 1700, John Douglas of Inchmarlo and Tilwhilly,—all in Kincardineshire.

The son, John Horne, was an advocate in Edinburgh, and succeeded his father in Westhall. Having added considerably to his estate, he obtained a charter from King William and Queen Mary, erecting the lands of Westhall, Petmedden, Ryhill, Ardoyne, Petmalchie, and Rayne into a free-barony, to be called the barony of Horne—the town of Old Rayne to be the burgh-of-barony of the same. A relic of this feudal dignity still stands in the centre of the village (which was in olden days a country-town of some importance, where stood a residence of the Bishop of Aberdeen, and where one of the largest fairs in the north, that of St. Lawrence, was and still is held in the month of August); being a granite pillar, standing on steps, to which the "jougs" were formerly attached. A portion of the chain which had secured that dreaded instrument of punishment was still to be seen, attached to the pillar, long within living memory. Mr. Horne was, along with Dundas of Arniston, also a Jacobite, the medium of communication between Henrietta Mordaunt, Duchess of Gordon, and the Society of Advocates, in certain negotiations respecting a medal which her Grace, in honour of the "Chevalier de St. George," had presented to the Society. This was in 1711, and the transaction, having a treasonable flavour about it, made some sensation at the time. John Horne married the Hon. Anna Arbuthnot, daughter of the second Viscount, by whom he had two daughters—Anne, who succeeded him, and Agnes, who died unmarried. Anne married, in 1714, Hew, second son of the Hon. Sir Hew Dalrymple of North Berwick, Bart., Lord President of the Session; third son of James, Viscount Stair, Lord President; and by him, who was afterwards a judge, with the title of Lord Drummore, had a large family. Their eldest son, General Robert Dalrymple-Horne, who commanded for many years the first Royals and saw much active service, married, in 1754, Mary, daughter and heiress of Sir James Elphinston, third Baronet of Logie-Elphinstone, who brought him that contiguous estate and residence, and her name along with it. Westhall, after this marriage, became deserted for the more commodious house of Logie, as, although Mr. James Horne had made some additions which still remain, the old house was straitened in its accommodation, and more extended ideas of comfort were coming in. John Horne had greatly beautified the place about the end of the seventeenth century; and, from the fine soil, the groves and stately avenues, stretching far in several different directions, showed, after a century of growth, a great extent of noble timber. This, however, was too valuable to be allowed to stand profitless to the owner; and only a few fine old trees now remain to show what Westhall might have been but for the ruthless axe of a bygone age.

General D. H. Elphinstone's grandson, the late Sir James D. H. Elphinstone, repaired and added to the old house about the year 1838, in his father's life-time, and took up his residence there. In 1860 it passed into the possession of Lady Leith of Freefield, who still further largely added to it. At Lady Leith's death, in 1883, it devolved on her stepson, General Disney Leith, C.B., who now possesses it.

THE END.

www.ingramcontent.com/pod-product-compliance
Lightning Source LLC
Chambersburg PA
CBHW081832170426
43199CB00017B/2711